Weighing up the Evidence

TIMELINE:

The Police

Elizabeth Campling

Dryad Press Limited London

F

Contents

Typeset by Tek-Art Ltd, Kent
and printed in Great Britain by
Anchor Press Ltd,
Tiptree, Essex,
for the Publishers
Dryad Press Limited,
4 Fitzhardinge Street,
London W1H 0AH

ISBN 0 8521 9789 6

ACKNOWLEDGMENTS

The author and publishers thank the following for their
kind permission to reproduce copyright illustrations:
BBC Hulton Picture Library, pages 18, 22, 46, 48; the
British Museum, page 10; Mary Evans Picture Library,
pages 24, 27, 28, 32, 33, 36, 41, 43; The Home Office,
page 54; Illustrated London News Picture Library,
page 45; the Mansell Collection, pages 5, 7, 12, 13; the
Press Association Ltd, page 49; Punch, page 55;
Sussex Police Archives, pages 38, 40, 52.

Front cover: *top* Metropolitan Police;
below left Illustrated London News Picture Library;
below right Mary Evans Picture Library.

Introduction

Ever since people came together in organized societies, long before written records began, it has been found necessary to control the actions of individuals for the good of the whole community. However much societies have differed in other ways, some actions were always singled out as anti-social. People who used unprovoked violence against their neighbours, who murdered or stole, or who were just unacceptably disruptive have nearly always been marked out for special disapproval and punishment. In addition, no society, however warlike, could function in the face of a widespread breakdown of law and order. Markets could not run if stallholders and customers brawled over each transaction, nor could the harvest be brought in if men with grudges fought each other over the farmers' fields. Preserving law and order also became seen as a vital function of any society.

Throughout history, therefore, societies have devised rules to govern conduct. These are the laws or customs of that society. However, no law is of much use unless it can be enforced. Someone has to identify law-breakers, arrest them and deliver them to justice. This is what we mean by the policing of society, although the actual term is a modern one that was not used in Britain until the late eighteenth century. How the police as we know them in Britain today evolved through the ages is the subject of this book.

The story is not straightforward. Because law and order is such a basic concern of any society, the police of a society are bound to mirror its values. In societies that claim to rest on the consent of the governed, the police are seen as servants of the community. The laws they enforce are those agreed on by the majority of citizens through their elected assemblies, and the powers of the police themselves are limited as well. This is the ideal that has been held up in Britain since the first modern police force was formed there in 1829, although reality may often have fallen short of it.

Societies in which the government or ruling class feels under threat from its own citizens have to be policed differently. Here the police have not only to deal with ordinary crime, but also to maintain state security by stamping out any opposition to the powers-that-be. In these circumstances they act as agents of the government rather than of society as a whole. This may result in ordinary police forces being given sweeping powers of detention and interrogation, as is the case in many dictatorships past and present, or in the formation of a separate "secret" or political police, such as the Soviet KGB, or the SAVAK of pre-revolutionary Iran, or the GESTAPO in Nazi Germany. Such forces are responsible to no one but the authorities they serve and inspire fear rather than respect.

Societies sometimes use their police to enforce moral codes, and this involves prying into the private lives of individuals. A short-lived experiment of this kind was made in seventeenth-century England. A modern example is the revolutionary police in present-day Iran, who enforce the Islamic moral code.

The status of the police is therefore intimately bound up with the society in which they operate and with the sort of things they are expected to do. Where there is reasonable agreement among people about the kind of laws they live under, the police tend to be popular and respected – except among hardened criminals, of course. Where there is widespread discontent with the existing system, antipathy to the police results, even if few people dare show it openly. This is tending to occur in the complex and divided society of modern Britain, where the comfortable old image of the local "Bobby", who is every good citizen's friend, has increasingly come under fire from some sections of the community.

The role of the police reflects the society around them in other ways as well. What they are asked to do and the way they are expected to do it are affected by many things – by technological progress, by changes in moral values and by political stresses at home and abroad. In recent decades, for example, the spread of international terrorism, the computer "information revolution" and the increased mobility of society have all changed the job of the British police into something their ancestors of a hundred years ago would barely recognize.

In the same way, the morale of the police themselves and the way they feel about their job depend on the value society places on them. The kind of people who join the police force, the training they receive and the enthusiasm and humanity with which they work from day to day are all bound up with this. This book looks both at the way in which British society has been policed over the ages and at the experiences of policemen and women themselves.

The British police of the 1980s are the result of a long and complex development through time, which is indissolubly linked with our history and culture. If our history had taken a different turn, the police as we know them today would have been different too. On pages 60-63 is a time-chart which shows highlights in the history of the police alongside major changes in society from ancient times to the present day. It should help you understand how the British police have developed over time.

On pages 58-59 is a list of the sources used in this book and suggestions for further reading. Drawing a picture of the British police at any given time is often far from easy. Many written records dating back to the ninth century have survived and the administrative history of our police can be traced without too much difficulty. From documents we can discover how law enforcement officers were appointed through the ages and what their powers and duties were. Discovering how the system worked in practice and how it was experienced by both the public and the police themselves involves, however, a tricky piece of detective work. Direct information is often scanty, although clues are sometimes given away incidentally in diaries and letters and even works of fiction – for law and order (or the lack of it) affected everyone's daily life very closely. At no time, however, can we be certain that the picture is anywhere near complete. Only in our own time does the evidence become more abundant and accessible.

The picture is most incomplete when it comes to reconstructing what ordinary policemen or women felt about their "lot". Throughout history constables have tended to be of lowly birth and little education. Until this century, few bothered to put their thoughts about their life and work on to paper. What it felt like to enforce the law in early times we can learn only partially and indirectly by reading between the lines. When we read in thirteenth-century parish records about the reluctance shown by ordinary men to serve as the local constable, or of attacks made on them by irate villagers, we learn something of what the job must have entailed, just as we can from the few surviving notebooks of semi-literate nineteenth-century rural policemen

In the past few years an intense debate has taken place in Britain about the proper role and responsibility of the police. This book should help you understand that this is not just an academic discussion but reflects the values and problems of society at large.

The Ancient World

Although this book is mostly about the history of the police in Britain, it begins with a survey of how law and order was kept in ancient times. We know next to nothing about how British society was run before about the ninth century AD but we do know that the British Isles had been invaded many times and influenced by many different cultural traditions, including policing ones. This chapter takes a brief look at some of them.

PRE-LITERATE SOCIETIES

As far as we can tell, in pre-literate societies, where the main bonds holding people together were those of kinship, the actions that were regarded as anti-social and the ways in which these were punished were passed down from generation to generation as tribal customs. Responsibility for catching the offender probably rested with the kinsman of the victim, who often had the right to take revenge on the whole family of the criminal. Such blood feuds might last for several generations. An example of this ancient system still in operation today is the Mafia.

THE MESOPOTAMIANS

Blood feuds are hardly an efficient way of policing society, for they usually cause more violence than they prevent. As societies became more sophisticated, they looked for better ways of controlling behaviour. Some literate societies developed written codes of law to help people live

The stone obelisk on which the laws of King Hammurabi were inscribed. At the top the king (on the left) is receiving instructions from the sun god, Shamash. This is one of the few definite pieces of evidence that have come down to us from ancient times about how societies then maintained law and order. Why has it survived?

together harmoniously. The earliest surviving one is that of King Hammurabi of Mesopotamia, who reigned from 1792 to 1750 BC. It covers a wide range of crimes from serious ones like murder, rape and theft to commercial sharp practices like watering down the beer and wine sold in taverns. Punishments were savage by modern standards. Burglars, for example, were to be sealed up in the wall of the house they had been caught robbing.

THE ANCIENT HEBREWS

Books of the Old Testament like Leviticus, Deuteronomy and parts of Exodus are records of the legal code of the ancient Hebrews.

Some Hebrew laws:

But if a man come presumptiously upon his neighbour to slay him with guile; thou shalt take him from mine altar that he may die. . .
But if men strive together, and one smite another with a stone, or with his fist, and he die not but keepeth to his bed;
If he rise again, and walk abroad upon his staff, then he that smote him be quit; only he shall pay for the loss of his time, and shall cause him to be thoroughly healed.

(*Source: The Bible*, Exodus 21:14, 18-19)

How did the Hebrews try to distinguish between different types of killing and the punishments for them?

THE GERMAN TRIBES

Not all ancient communities were as well-organized or as literate as this, but even the most primitive evolved rough and ready ways of keeping the peace and finding alternatives to the blood feud. The Roman historian Tacitus, writing in the first century AD, has left us a fascinating account of how the uncouth and uncultured (in Tacitus's view) German tribes of his day conducted their affairs.

Keeping the peace in the German tribes:

It is incumbent to take up a father's feuds or a kinsman's not less than his friendships; but such feuds do not continue unappeasable; even homicide is atoned for by a fixed number of cattle or sheep, and the whole family thereby receives satisfaction, to the public advantage; for feuds are dangerous side by side with liberty.

(*Source:* Tacitus, *Germania*, Penguin, 1970)

In what ways did the three societies above try to find a way to make blood feuds and private vengeance unnecessary? How did their systems of justice differ?

Unfortunately, we have much less information about how these laws were enforced and who was responsible for identifying offenders and catching them. It seems to have depended mostly on a particular society's military traditions. Some states kept a regular or "standing" army of professional soldiers and these were often used for police duties as well. Hammurabi, for example, made his soldiers responsible for catching thieves. In Hebrew and Germanic society there were no professional soldiers. It was the duty of every able-bodied man to take up arms when necessary. It was natural, therefore, for responsibility for law and order to also fall on the male community as a whole. In small tribal societies, where everyone knew everyone else and shared the same values, such a system probably worked quite well most of the time.

THE ROMAN EMPIRE

The Romans had a complex written code of law of which they were very proud. As the Roman Empire spread, Roman law had to be imposed on societies with very different traditions, who were often resentful of foreign domination. Usually, conquered peoples were allowed to keep and administer their own customs, so long as these did not conflict with Roman law. If crimes were committed that undermined Roman authority, such as the murder of public officials or acts of riot and rebellion, then Rome's formidable professional army, recruited from all areas of the Empire, acted as policeman. A famous example of this can be seen in the events surrounding the trial and execution of Christ. When Jesus was first brought before the Governor, Pontius Pilate, he ruled that the matter was outside his jurisdiction, as no offence had been committed against Roman law. Under intense pressure from Jewish religious leaders, however, Pilate gave in and condemned Jesus to death. After that, the task of guarding him and leading him to execution fell to the Roman soldiers.

THE DARK AGES

In the fifth and sixth centuries AD the Roman Empire collapsed under the impact of waves of Barbarian invasions from the east. Europe broke up

A nineteenth-century artist's impression of the flogging of Boudicca, a British leader who rebelled against Roman rule in c.60 AD. Who do you think took the role of policeman here? Why do you think there are no contemporary pictures of this or similar events?

once again into small tribal communities, and records from this time – sometimes known as the "Dark Ages" – are very fragmentary. What little we can discover indicates that the old tribal system of family and community responsibility revived. The wild Vikings of Scandinavia left no written laws, but some of their literature has survived. *The Vinland Sagas* tell the story of their discovery of North America five centuries before Columbus. At one point in the account we read how Leif Eriksson hears rumours that his sister, Freydis, has committed some treacherous murders. In this case, however, the system of family responsibility does not work too well, as Leif has too much else on his mind.

A murderess escapes punishment:

He seized three of Freydis' men and tortured them into revealing everything that had happened; their stories tallied exactly. "I do not have the heart", said Leif, "to punish my sister Freydis as she deserves. But I prophesy that her descendants will never prosper."

(*Source: The Vinland Sagas*, Penguin, 1965)

SUMMARY Finding out about everyday matters like crime and punishment in ancient societies is a tricky piece of detective work. The evidence must be pieced together from a variety of different sources. Even then we have only fragments of the picture and cannot be sure that we have not missed something quite important simply because the evidence for it has disappeared. We can be fairly certain, however, that specialized police forces of the type we are familiar with today did not exist in ancient times. In small close-knit communities, keeping the peace was the responsibility of all able-bodied adult males, whereas in more complex societies like the Roman Empire the army often acted as policemen. Both systems must have had grave disadvantages. Soldiers acting as policemen were probably often brutal and arbitrary, but community policing was probably inefficient and often unjust. Families would close ranks to protect one of their own even if his or her guilt was obvious. On the other hand, there was ample scope for paying off old scores, and community law enforcement could easily tip over into mob violence and the hounding of innocent men whose only crime was to be different. A modern term for this would be *lynching*.

ON REFLECTION:

Why could ancient societies police themselves in a way that might not be possible today?

What advantages and disadvantages did such a system have?

What historical examples can you think of where communities took the law into their own hands at the expense of unpopular or non-conformist individuals? Does it ever happen today?

Anglo-Saxon Times to the Sixteenth Century

In 410 AD the Romans left Britain and the orderly society they had imposed fell apart. In the years that followed, waves of settlers from mainland Europe migrated to Britain and settled there permanently, creating a patchwork of small kingdoms and pushing the original Celtic inhabitants into remote areas on the fringes of the island like Cornwall and West Wales. The most numerous of the new peoples, the Angles and the Saxons, eventually gave their name to a period of English history that lasted from around 450 AD until the Norman conquest in 1066. The Normans then imposed an alien, French-speaking ruling class on their new subjects, but in time the two cultures merged to create the English language and culture we know today.

THE ANGLO-SAXONS We know little of how the early Anglo-Saxons ran their affairs. A farming people of Germanic origin, they had probably brought with them the tradition of family responsibility for law and order described by Tacitus. Over the centuries, however, their society became more sophisticated. One by one the kingdoms were converted to Christianity and a new class of literate churchmen came to play an active role in government and encouraged the development of written records and laws. The Church also discouraged the violence endemic in Anglo-Saxon society and condemned outright the customs of personal vengeance and private warfare. When England was finally united under King Alfred in the ninth century, the character of his government owed much both to its Germanic heritage and to the civilizing influence of the Church.

Although the new kingdom was hardly ever at peace and suffered frequent raids from the Vikings, particular attention was paid to the creation of a law-abiding community. According to Anglo-Saxon justice, each person had a value and anyone found guilty of murder had to pay a set amount of compensation, or *wergild*, to the victim's family. There was a lesser scale of fines for non-fatal injury. The job of apprehending the suspect fell first upon the family and then, as time went on, upon the local community as a whole. Each adult male over twelve had to be enrolled in a group of about ten families called a *tything*, headed by a *tythingman* chosen from among them. Tythings were then grouped into larger units known as *hundreds* and hundreds into *shires*. Each member of the tything was held responsible for the good behaviour of all the others. If one of them committed a crime, it was the duty of all the others to bring him before the courts. If they failed to do so, they were liable for a fine or confiscation of their goods. Although women were considered legally responsible for their actions and could pay and receive *wergild*, the whole administration of justice, from pursuit to punishment, was a male preserve and continued to be so for many centuries.

From where did the Anglo-Saxons inherit the wergild *system?*

In what way has the idea of one person standing as guarantor for another's good behaviour come down into the present-day English legal system?

Sometimes, of course, the suspect tried to escape. Then every man in the neighbourhood was required to down tools and chase the criminal until he or she was caught. This was known as the *hue and cry*.

A criminal is caught in Anglo-Saxon England, from a tenth-century manuscript. What are the other men in the picture doing? What sort of people are they?

What to do when a criminal runs away:

That men go without delay in pursuit of thieves: if the need is urgent, one is to inform the man in charge of the hundred, and he then the men over the tythings; and all are to go forth, where God may guide them, that they may reach the thief. . .
Further, we decree, if one hundred follows up a trail into another hundred, that is to be made known to the man in charge of that hundred, and he is then to go with them. If he neglects to do it, he is to pay 30 shillings to the King.
If anyone evades the law and flees, he who supported him in that injury is to pay compensation.
And if he is accused of abetting his escape, he is to clear himself according to as it is established in the district.

(*Source:* The Laws of King Athelstan, 926-930 AD)

Do you think that the instructions about taking up the hue and cry would have been very popular? If not, why not?

GUILT AND INNOCENCE

Once a suspect was caught, assessing guilt or innocence was also a local matter. All hundreds and shires were required to hold regular courts, or *moots*, at which suspects could be presented for trial by their fellow villagers. An official called the *shire reeve*, or *sheriff*, was appointed by the king to supervise the running of local courts and ensure fair play.

In what way can the sheriff be seen as an exception to the Anglo-Saxon custom of making law-enforcement a community responsibility?

One of the jobs of the modern police is to collect evidence against the accused to present at the trial. In Anglo-Saxon times more rough and ready methods were used. The accused were sometimes allowed to bring witnesses to swear to their good character or might have to undergo *trial by ordeal*. This involved being lowered, bound, into some water or being made to carry a red-hot iron in the hand for a distance of nine feet. If the suspect floated, or if the burn festered, those signs were considered to be evidence of guilt. If, however, the hand was healing cleanly after three days, or if the person sank, he or she was declared innocent. The results of the trial were believed to reflect God's judgement on the accused.

Establishing guilt or innocence:

If anyone pledges to undergo the ordeal, he is to come three days before to the mass-priest whose duty it is to consecrate it [the trial] and live off bread, water, salt and vegetables until he shall go to it, and be present at mass on each of these three days and go to communion on the day on which he shall go to the ordeal, and swear then the oath that he is guiltless of the charge . . . before he goes to the ordeal. And if it is of water, he is to sink one and a half ells on the rope; if it is of iron, it is to be three days before the hand is unbound.

(*Source:* The Laws of Athelstan, 926-930 AD)

Who do you think is responsible for supervising trial by ordeal?

What measures are laid down to ensure that the results are as fair as possible, according to the beliefs of the time?

ON REFLECTION:

We do not know how effective the Anglo-Saxon system was at catching criminals once a crime had been committed. It was probably more effective at preventing crime in the first place. Can you explain why this should have been?

MEDIEVAL BRITAIN After 1066 the new Norman rulers took over much of the old Anglo-Saxon system of law enforcement. Only the names sometimes changed now that French was the language of the ruling class. In the laws issued by King Henry I (1100–1135), for example, a tything was renamed a *frankpledge*. Over the next four turbulent centuries, however, as society changed, many changes also took place in the legal system. Crime ceased to be regarded as an offence against an individual and his family, which could be made good by compensation. Instead it was seen as an offence against the *King's Peace*. *Wergild* was replaced by punishments like death or mutilation, which were intended to deter others from committing the same crime. In

Men in prison and in the stocks, from a twelfth-century manuscript. Who would have been responsible for carrying out these punishments?

the eleventh century, the Church, whose influence in government was still great, turned against trial by ordeal, and this was gradually replaced in England by the *jury system*, by which suspects were judged by a panel of twelve reliable local men. Local courts lost their jurisdiction over serious cases, or *felonies*, which were tried by royal judges travelling around the country on circuit, as they still do today. They held courts called *Assizes*. The custom of communal fines and holding men personally responsible for the behaviour of their neighbours died out.

THE VILLAGE CONSTABLE

Yet the idea lived on, that catching offenders was a social duty that fell on the shoulders of every adult male. In an age of primitive communications, when even an experienced rider travelling light could not get from Northumberland to London in under six days, there was really no alternative. By the thirteenth century, each village, or *parish*, was required to appoint one of their number to bear special responsibility for seeing that these duties were carried out properly. These officials were given the Norman title of *constable*. Their duties included making sure that the hue and cry worked properly, guarding prisoners until their trial, and carrying out punishments for minor offences such as selling underweight bread or spreading malicious gossip. Constables were not paid, although they could sometimes claim expenses. Anyone who refused to serve was to incur a fine or even a period of imprisonment.

Catching criminals in the eleventh century:

That the hue and cry be followed according to the ancient use, so that all who neglect and refuse to follow it shall be taken into custody as abettors of the wrongdoers, and shall be delivered up to the Sheriff. Moreover, in every township, let four or six men be chosen according to its size, to follow the hue and cry hastily and swiftly, and to pursue the wrongdoers, if need be, with bows and arrows and other light arms, which shall be

provided at the common cost of the township and remain ever for the use thereof. And to this end let a free and lawful man be chosen from the most powerful in each hundred, who shall oversee the work and see that the aforesaid watches and pursuits be rightly carried out.

(*Source:* Royal Writ of 1253 for Watch and Ward)

The constable is not mentioned by name in the extract above but it is not too difficult to work out who he was and what his duties were. You will notice that the system has become more sophisticated since Anglo-Saxon times. In what ways?

Why was it necessary to coerce men into serving as constables by threatening to punish them if they refused?

Corrupt and inefficient constables:

Court records indicate that a tremendous amount of crime went unpunished throughout the Middle Ages. The phrases "the constable testifies that they are not to be found" or "the constable testifies that he slipped away" recur time after time. One particularly irksome problem was the right of suspects to seek sanctuary in a church, from which they could not be removed by force. After forty days there, they could go abroad unmolested.

Roger Pygburd was found killed in his bed in Eblesburn. Susan his wife first found him. The constable went for her but she fled to Bishopstone church, confessed to having killed Roger and abjured the realm [left the country].

(*Source:* The Wiltshire Assize of 1249)

Sometimes royal officials carried out a *Trailbaston*. This was a special investigation into what was going on in a particular area (rather like the commissions today that bring in someone from outside to look into local controversies). From them we can often find out a good deal about the state of law and order in the area. In 1306 a *Trailbaston* was held in the

Derbyshire Peak District, and the officials were asked to make careful inquiries:

7. Concerning those who hinder the constables, bailiffs and other ministers of our lord the king from performing their office as they have been charged by our lord the king to do to keep the peace of his land.
8. Concerning those who are constables or bailiffs of our lord the king and have their warrant to attach felons and disturbers of his peace but take gifts or through friendships or for any other reasons, let the felons go or have them warned in advance, so that the king's commands can in no wise be carried out.

(*Source:* Report of the 1306 Trailbaston in the Derbyshire Peak District)

What reasons are given here for villains being able to escape justice in medieval England? What reasons might there be other than the ones mentioned?

THE JUSTICES OF THE PEACE

A New Boss:

Medieval sheriffs were often very corrupt. The character of the wicked Sheriff of Nottingham in the Robin Hood legend probably has its roots here. A law passed in the reign of Edward III (1327-77) stripped the sheriffs of many of their duties and transferred these to local people. Henceforth reliable local landowners were to serve as unpaid *Justices of the Peace* enforcing law and order in their area. JPs were to hold their own courts, known as Quarter Sessions, to try minor offences. These superseded the hundred courts, which gradually became defunct. Village constables were to work under the justices, and any new duties assigned to JPs were also those of the constables, who were responsible for seeing that they were carried out.

First, that for the keeping of the peace, there shall be assigned in each county of England one lord and with him three or four of the most worthy men of the county . . . and they shall have the power to restrain evil doers, rioters and all other miscreants; to pursue, arrest and capture and chastise them according to their trespass or offence; to have them imprisoned and duly punished according to the law and custom of the kingdom.

(*Source:* Justices of the Peace Act, 1361)

THE WARS OF THE ROSES

To make sure that a system that left so much power in local hands was not abused required a vigilant and strong-minded king. When royal authority was weak, as it often was during a minority or when the king was fighting abroad, law and order could all too easily break down. This happened in the fifteenth century during the Wars of the Roses, when the succession to the throne was disputed between two rival factions — York and Lancaster. Taking advantage of the chaos, some powerful landowners, known as "overmighty subjects", gathered bands of armed followers or *retainers* and terrorized whole neighbourhoods.

Law and order break down:

[the faithful Commons tell of] great and lamentable complaints of your true poor subjects, universally throughout every part of this your realm, of robberies, ravishments, extortions, oppressions, riots, unlawful assemblies, wrongful imprisonments done unto them. . . . And the said misdoers be so favoured by persons of great might . . . that they disturb and hinder your Justices and constables in every part of this your realm, that no execution of your law may be had.

(*Source:* Rolls of Parliament, 1459)

The JPs were usually small landowners and the constables simple villagers. Why would they find it difficult to bring an overmighty subject and his retainers to justice?

THE TOWNS Between 1066 and 1485 internal and international trade expanded, and more people in England began to live in towns. By 1377 London had a population of 23,314. Bristol, the next largest city, had 6,345. Towns presented new law and order problems. They attracted the restless, for whom village life was too restricting. Fairs and markets gave numerous opportunities for brawling, while in seaports the presence of foreign merchants and sailors frequently led to racial tensions. Most important of all, perhaps, towns lacked the community spirit of the villages, where everyone knew everyone else and some anti-social behaviour could be kept in check by community disapproval. In the towns it was all too easy for the would-be criminal to disappear into the anonymity of the crowd. The major crisis of law and order in the towns was not to begin until the sixteenth century, but even in medieval times the matter caused concern.

When villages grew into towns, they usually kept their old customs and the towns-people elected constables from among their number. However, it soon became clear that stronger methods were needed.

Policing the towns:

And for the greater security of the country the king has commanded that in the great towns, which are enclosed, the gates be shut from sunset until sunrise . . . and from henceforth watches be kept . . . in every city by six men at every gate; and in every borough by twelve men; in every town by six men or four according to the number of the inhabitants . . . and that they keep watch continually all night from sunset to sunrise. And if any stranger pass them by, he shall be arrested until morning and if no suspicion be found he shall go quit then. . . . And if they will not suffer themselves to be arrested, hue and cry shall be levied against them, and those who keep watch shall follow with all the town from town to town, until they be taken.

(*Source:* Statute of Winchester, 1285)

What additional method is laid down here for keeping the peace in the towns?

From what sort of people would the watchmen be chosen?

ON REFLECTION:

In what ways does the English policing system change between the ninth and the fifteenth centuries and in what ways does it remain the same? What historical reasons can you find for any changes and similarities you may have noticed?

Nowadays we have a professional police force but some features of the medieval idea of community responsibility live on in our legal system today. What are they?

The Sixteenth and Seventeenth Centuries

These two centuries cover the reigns of the Tudor and Stuart monarchs, during which momentous changes took place in English political and social life. The influence of Parliament, especially of the House of Commons, increased. Under Henry VIII, England broke with the Roman Catholic Church and set up the Church of England with the king at its head. The monasteries were closed down and despoiled. In 1536 Wales was formally joined to England and copied the English system of local government. In response to a rising demand for wool on the international market, many big landowners turned their estates over to sheep-rearing. Many tenant farmers were evicted and ordinary labourers lost their jobs. The civil war fought between king and Parliament from 1642-49 ended in the execution of Charles I and eleven years of republican government – the Commonwealth – under Oliver Cromwell. The monarchy was restored in 1660 but another king, James II, was deposed in the "Glorious Revolution" of 1688, which permanently strengthened the power of Parliament and the landowning class. In other ways, though, life changed very little. Most people still lived in the countryside. Communications from one part of the country to another were still primitive and slow. The government in London had no real alternative to relying on local people to administer most of their own affairs.

The first Tudor kings, Henry VII and Henry VIII, re-established royal authority and curbed the powers of the overmighty barons. To do this they relied heavily on the support of the middle rank of landowners and merchants, who had most to gain from civil peace and most to lose from disorder. The Justices of the Peace became the main props of local government, including the maintenance of law and order. Constables were ordered to present reports or *presentments* of the state of law and order in the area to the Quarter Sessions.

A TIME OF SOCIAL UPHEAVAL The sixteenth century was a time of intense social strains. The Reformation brought religious conflict, as a sizeable minority of Englishmen and women refused to accept the new Church of England. Closure of the monasteries deprived the poor of institutions that had given out charity and medical care in hard times. Enclosures threw men out of work. Many became beggars and some turned to crime. The situation was made worse by a series of exceptionally bad harvests in the 1590s. Social historians who have tried to reconstruct this period from scattered records have come to the conclusion that petty lawlessness and violence began to rise steadily during the reign of Elizabeth 1 (1559-1603), to reach a peak between the 1590s and 1620. In an attempt to bring the situation under control, a flood of new legislation was passed, penalizing a wide range of people, from those who did not attend Sunday worship at the Church of England to the unemployed vagrants or "sturdy beggars" who tramped England's roads. The job of enforcing the new laws fell on the JPs and their constables, who added it

The Ducking Stool, from an early seventeenth-century engraving. This was the traditional punishment meted out to women accused of spreading malicious gossip. What can we learn from this picture about the man actually carrying out the punishment, who may have been the local constable?

to the duties they already had. There were frequent appeals to the Queen from overworked country justices who claimed that their backs were being "broken" under the "stacks of statutes" that had been laid upon them. The same must have been true for their constables.

With one brief interruption during the Commonwealth period, the system continued unaltered through all the political upheavals of the seventeenth century, and we can study the period as a whole, only bearing in mind that the job of constable or justice must have been even more difficult than usual during times of civil war.

THE CONSTABLE

A seventeenth-century constable's oath:

You shall swear that you shall well and truly serve the King's Majesty in the office of Constable of this town and you shall see that the peace of Our Sovereign Lord . . . be well and duly kept according to your power . . . [and] shall arrest all that you see doing Riots, making Affrays or otherwise breaking of the Peace. And you shall do your best endeavour that the Statute of Winchester for Hue and Cry and the Statute made for the punishment of Rogues, vagabonds, Sturdy Beggars and Idle Persons be all put in due execution. You shall apprehend such as use unlawful games and duly execute all Precepts and Process sent to you by the mayor of this town and present all Bloodshed, Outcries and Affrays . . . committed within the precincts of this Town and perform all things belonging to the Office of Constable to do to your power. So help you God.

(*Source: The Book of Oaths*, Portsmouth City Archives, quoted in *A History of the Police in Portsmouth*, Portsmouth Papers No. 2, published by the City Council, 1967)

A constable's duties:

For keeping of Erasmus Townsend and
his wife, Joshua Blauge and David Lafown,
4 nights each   5s.   4d.

for five locks for their hand bolts and
fetters   4s.   6d.
For clean straw   9d.

(*Source:* the expenses claimed by Constable Alexander fforbes of Portsmouth for 8 May 1694, quoted in *The Portsmouth Papers*)

For whipping a man   6d.
For whipping a man and his wife   1s.   0d.
For carrying a Hue and Cry to Gosport   2d.

(*Source:* the expenses claimed by Constable Edmonds of Portsmouth for 10 October 1698)

What do the oath and the expense sheets tell us about the duties of a constable in the sixteenth and seventeenth centuries?

Why do the constables need to claim expenses? How does this differ from what is required of a modern policeman or woman?

An unpopular job:

The job of constable was time-consuming and made serious inroads into the time a man could give to earning his living. For simple farmers who often lived at subsistence level, this was a grave drawback. Being a constable also tended to put a man on bad terms with his neighbours, for many of the new regulations were very unpopular. This must have had an effect on the quality of the service that most local constables provided. In 1618 the Portsmouth constables were fined for "neglecting their office and not punishing vagabonds, rogues and minstrels for staying in the town contrary to the statute". In *Much Ado about Nothing* and *Measure for Measure* Shakespeare included idle and reluctant constables as comic figures.

DOGBERRY (the head constable)   You shall also make no noise in the streets; for the watch to battle and to talk is most tolerable [intolerable] and not to be endured.
SECOND WATCHMAN   We will rather sleep than talk; we know what belongs to a watch.
DOGBERRY   Why, you speak like an ancient and most quiet watchman, for I cannot see how sleeping would offend; only have a care that your bills be not stolen. Well, you are to call at all the alehouses and bid those that are drunk get them to bed.
WATCH   How if they will not.
DOGBERRY   Why, then let them alone till they are sober. . .
WATCH   Well, sir.
DOGBERRY   If you meet a thief, you may suspect him, by virtue of your office, to be no true man; and, for such kind of men, the less you meddle or make with them, why, the more is for your honesty.

(*Source: Much Ado About Nothing*, Act 3, scene 3, lines 25-45)

In 1573 William Bullein wrote a satirical pamphlet, in the form of a dialogue between a citizen (called by the Latin name of *Civis*) and his wife (Latin: *Uxor*), about the poor state of law and order in England.

UXOR   What number of men in harness are these? Some sleeping, and many of them seemeth to go whispering together, and behind them there appeareth other men putting forth their heads out of corners, wearing no harness.

CIVIS   These are not only the constables with the watchmen in London, but also almost throughout this realm, most falsely abusing the time, coming very late to the watch, sitting down in some common place of watching, wherein some falleth asleep by reason of labour or much drinking before, or else nature requireth rest in the night. These fellows think every hour a thousand until they go home, home, home, every man to bed.

(*Source: A Dialogue of Pestilence*, by William Bullein, 1573)

Concealing an offence:

As simple countrymen themselves, constables often had more sympathy with fellow villagers driven to crime by poverty than they had with the authorities. When the constable of one Wiltshire village discovered stolen corn in the house of a certain Thomas Morris, Morris entreated him "to be good unto him and his children or else he would be utterly undone". As a result, the constable, Robert Toomer, "moved with pity, sought his neighbours that this business might be concealed".

(*Source: English Society 1580-1680*, Keith Wrightson, Hutchinson, 1982)

Wrightson's book is an example of a new sort of history in which historians attempt to put together a detailed picture of everyday life by a thorough investigation of all the scattered and incomplete records. What other reason might constable Toomer have had for concealing the theft?

THE COMMON-WEALTH EXPERIMENT

The Commonwealth decade was a time of experiment, as men tried to find ways of governing the country without a king. England's new rulers were Puritans, who saw it as their mission to make the country more godly and to wipe out immoral behaviour. To make it easier to enforce strict Puritan morals on everyone else and also to guard against a royalist uprising, Oliver Cromwell, the Lord Protector, divided the country into eleven districts, each of which was under the control of an army officer of the rank of Major-General. Each had at his disposal a troop of trained, professional soldiers, whose pay came from fines levied on royalists. Local justices and constables were expected to co-operate with them without argument. This experiment was regarded as an attack on the right of local people to manage their own affairs and proved very unpopular. It was abandoned after two years.

The duties of the Major-Generals:

They shall in their constant Carriage and Conservation, encourage and

promote Godliness and Virtue, and Discourage and Discountenance all
Profaneness and Ungodliness; and shall endeavour with the other
Justices of the Peace . . . that the Laws against Drunkenness,
Blaspheming, and taking the Name of God in vain, by swearing and
cursing, Plays and Interludes, and prophaning the Lord's day, and such
like wickedness and abominations, be put in more effectual execution
than they have been hitherto.

(*Source:* instructions to the Major-Generals, *Writings and Speeches of Oliver Cromwell*,
Harvard University Press, 1937-47)

What sort of behaviour did Cromwell regard as "ungodly"?

*Does this give us another reason, apart from the one given above, why this
experiment should have been so unpopular?*

THE TOWNS   Towns continued to expand throughout this period and to attract the
rootless, the restless and those with something to hide. By 1650 London
had 200,000 inhabitants. Poverty was widespread and crime of all sorts
flourished. The parish of Southwark, south of the Thames, was so
notorious as a haunt of thieves that no honest man dared set foot there. It
even housed a well-known school for training young boys in the art of
picking pockets. As always, when so many people were packed so closely
together, emotions often ran high and frequent riots were another
common problem.

Disorder in the city:

. . . that night I returned to London and found all the wards full of
watchers, the cause thereof was for that very near the Theatre or Curtain
at the time of the plays there lay a prentice sleeping in the grass and one
Challes alias Grostock did turn the toe upon the belly of the same
prentice, whereupon the apprentice start up and after words they fell to
plain blows. The company soon increased of both sides to the number of
five hundred at the least.

(*Source:* a letter from William Fleetwood, the City Recorder, to Lord Burghley, 18 June
1584)

*Among which group of people and in what circumstance did this riot break
out?*

Are there any obvious modern equivalents?

The first professionals:

As the old system of *watch and ward* showed itself increasingly unable to
cope with the growing law and order problem in the cities, a new idea was
introduced during the reign of Charles II (1660-85). In 1663 London
appointed paid watchmen to patrol the streets from sunset to sunrise.
There were 1,000 of them; they were paid about one shilling per night

Watchmen, as depicted in an early seventeenth-century book illustration. How would these watchmen have been appointed and how are they equipped?

(about the same as an unskilled labourer), carried a bell (so that they could summon help from the citizens), a staff and a lantern, and were nicknamed "Charlies" after the king. The calibre of men applying to be watchmen was very low and the experiment was not a great success.

Wanted, men for London watchmen. None need apply for this lucrative situation without being the age of 60, 70, 80 or 90 years; blind with one eye, and seeing very little with the other; crippled with one or both legs; deaf as a post; with an asthmatical cough that tears them in pieces; whose speed will keep pace with a snail, and the strength of whose arm would be able to arrest an old washerwoman of fourscore returning from a hard-day's fag at the wash-tub.

(*Source:* anonymous poster which appeared in London in the 1690s)

In what way were the Charlies a break with the English policing tradition as it had developed up to the seventeenth century?

What indications do we have that the system did not work too well right from the beginning? Why did the calibre of the Charlies tend to be so low?

To what modern expression has the nickname "Charley" given rise?

SUMMARY In most respects, the system of law enforcement remained unchanged from the ninth to the eighteenth century, even though England was becoming an increasingly populous and complex society. In spite of obvious defects in the system, Englishmen remained attached to the idea of policing and justice as an unpaid community responsibility, even if they were usually reluctant to perform those duties in practice. The powerful landowning class, in particular, saw the local policing system as protection against too much royal power and interference from London. Anything else, such as the experiment with the Major-Generals, smacked of a threat to their "liberties".

ON REFLECTION:

Can you think of any circumstances that might arise to persuade the English landowning class to change their minds and decide that a professional police force would be worth risking some of their "liberties" for?

The evidence we have indicates that the idea of a proper police force was unpopular with ordinary people as well, even though they were often the victims of crime. Why should this be?

1700 – 1829

The eighteenth century is generally regarded as a dark age of crime and social deprivation in England. The population almost doubled from five and a half to nine million. As the industrial revolution got underway, small towns like Birmingham, Manchester and Leeds grew into grim industrial cities which swallowed up the surrounding countryside and lacked most of the basic amenities for a healthy life. The agricultural revolution improved the productivity of farming but, at the same time, drove thousands of people off the land and into vagrancy, theft or poaching. With the building of the first turnpike roads, travel between major population centres became easier and quicker, but also more dangerous, for armed highwaymen roamed the roads leading in and out of large towns and attacked and robbed travellers. It is hardly surprising, therefore, that the system of amateur policing broke down almost entirely and that the first experiments were made in London with full-time professional policemen. The period covered by this chapter ended with the formation of the Metropolitan Police, the first of the modern police forces.

A VIOLENT SOCIETY

No new system of local government was set up to cope with the new distribution of population. The expanding towns merely took over the age-old customs of the villages they engulfed, including the unpaid parish constable, who was totally inadequate for the job in hand. As late as 1811, for example, Liverpool, a seaport of 100,000 inhabitants, had no police at all by day and only a few feeble watchmen by night. As always, things were at their worst in London. As thousands drifted there in search of a better life, the city spread far outside its old boundaries into the adjoining county

The Watch Discovers a Naughty Couple, a print by Hogarth, c. 1720. Watchmen in towns would have been much more likely to uncover this sort of offence than to catch really hardened and dangerous criminals.

of Middlesex and swallowed up over a hundred once-rural parishes. Problems were made worse by a high level of drunkenness among all ages, encouraged by the sale of cheap gin. In 1750 there was one public house for every fifteen houses in the City of London, and one to every five in the neighbouring area of Holborn. Drunkenness bred further crime and deprivation. Paintings by Hogarth give a vivid picture of the squalor and disorder that was eighteenth-century London.

Disorder in the towns:

November 20th 1729. Riot at Pudshole	3s	4d
November 25th. Hue and Cry for robbing at Salisbury	4s	6d
December 27th. Murder: Taking the Dutchman – spent on ye guard.	5s	8d
December 31st. Paid for laying out and watching three nights ye Dead Man, candles	4s	8d
January 20th 1730. A Riot at ye Three Compasses	3s	6d
April 2nd. A Riot in ye Butcher Row	3s	4d
April 20th. A Hue and Cry: a horse stolen – Sussex	4s	2d

(*Source:* bill for expenses submitted by Constables Garth and Stevens of the parish of Portsea on the outskirts of Portsmouth for the period September 1729 to September 1730, Portsmouth City Archives, published in *The Portsmouth Papers, no. 2*)

What picture does this give us of life in an eighteenth-century city?

What unexpected job were the constables given in December?

There was little understanding in the eighteenth century of the causes of crime and its possible link with poverty and ignorance. No distinction was made between hardened, dangerous criminals and gangs, and those who had been driven to crime by destitution, including many women and orphaned children. The landowners who dominated Parliament could think of no better solution than to inflict severe punishments for even minor crimes. Between 1680 and 1820 the number of offences carrying the death penalty rose from 50 to over 200. They included such trivial crimes against property as stealing a shilling or scribbling graffiti on Westminster Bridge.

CONSTABLES AND WATCHMEN In the circumstances, the job of constable or watchman became more unpopular than ever and in the towns it was often downright dangerous. Those who could afford to usually purchased exemption. Daniel Defoe, the author, for example, paid £10 in 1721 to be excused from the office of constable in Stoke Newington in North London, where he lived. Those who could not avoid it seldom did the job with much enthusiasm. The London Charlies were by now a joke and were often the butt of horseplay at the hands of gangs of wealthy, idle young men, who amused themselves poking elderly watchmen with their swords or tripping them up.

Reluctant constables:

Officers of justice have owned to me that they have passed by such criminals with the warrants in their pockets against them without daring to apprehend them; and, indeed, they could not be blamed for not exposing themselves to sure destruction; for it is a melancholy truth that, at this very day, a rogue no sooner gives the alarm, within certain purlieus, than twenty or thirty armed villains are found ready to come to his assistance.

(*Source:* diary of Henry Fielding, Bow Street magistrate, 1751)

Why were ordinary constables in London so unwilling to do their job properly? Can you blame them?

Can you suggest any ways in which constables might be induced to do their job more conscientiously?

What sort of law-breakers were likely to get caught most often in eighteenth-century England?

Constables commended:

There were some constables who took their work seriously, although they were probably the exception. In April 1799 the *Hampshire Telegraph* reported how the Portsmouth constables, "by their extraordinary activity and vigilance", caught a gang of notorious criminals led by "Shepton Mallet Jack", who had stolen £100 from a guest at the Fountain Inn.

and what is further to their credit, although the offenders had taken different routes, to the distance of 8 or 9 miles, nearly the whole of the money was recovered and restored to its owner.

(*Source: The Hampshire Telegraph*, 27 April 1799)

From examining the available evidence, we get the impression that conscientious constables were the exception rather than the rule. Was this necessarily true, or can we sometimes be misled by the evidence? To help you answer this, think about the impression someone living in the future would get of our present society if the only evidence available was back-copies of The Sun, *or criminal court records. Would these give an accurate impression of what life was like for most people? This does not mean that there is no point in trying to reconstruct the past from the evidence which is left to us, but merely that we should always be aware that our picture may be incomplete and be prepared to adjust our views if fresh evidence turns up.*

SELF-HELP In the absence of an effective police force, those who could afford it took measures for their own protection. Country gentlemen slept with pistols under their pillows and employed gamekeepers to guard their lands against poachers. Townsmen went about surrounded by armed servants "even at noon, as if one were going into battle" (Horace Walpole, 1752). In some affluent suburbs, such as Toxteth in Liverpool and Landport in Portsmouth, householders clubbed together and employed their own watchmen.

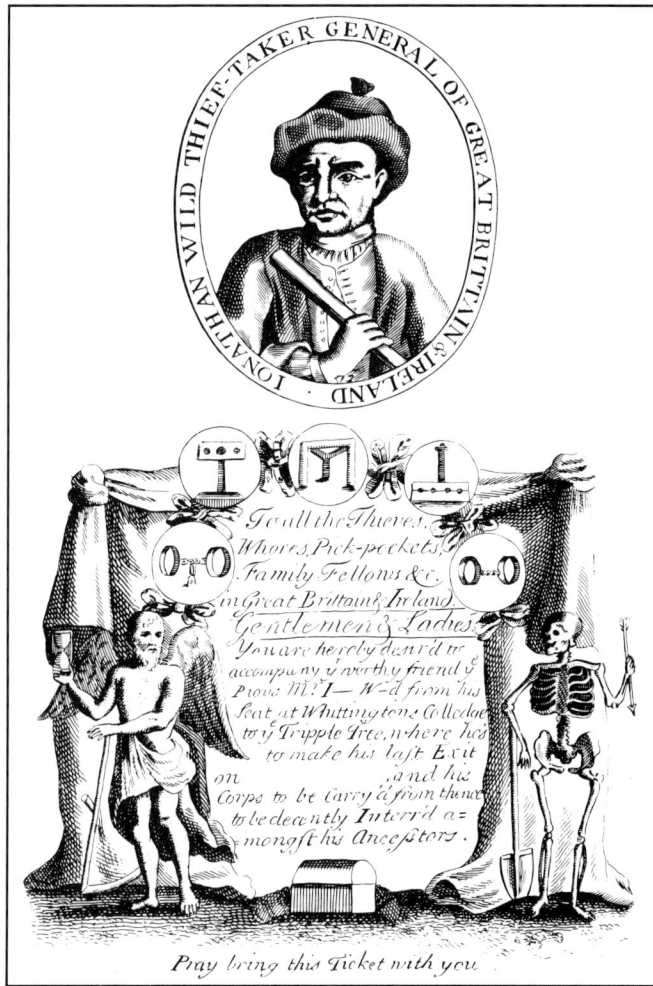

An invitation to the execution of Jonathan Wild. Why were "fences" like Wild able to flourish in eighteenth-century towns?

Wealthy people who had been robbed often offered rewards for the recovery of their property, and some enterprising rogues made a living out of earning them. The most notorious was Jonathan Wild, who advertised himself as "Thief-Taker General". First he would order his men to commit a burglary and then very courteously, feigning complete ignorance of the theft, restore the goods to their rightful owner on payment of the reward. He made a good living for seven years before he was eventually caught and hanged. As usual, the poor, who were often the victims of crime themselves (although most of it went unrecorded), managed as best they could.

NEW IDEAS ABOUT LAW AND ORDER

By the second half of the century some thoughtful people were questioning the whole basis of England's system of law enforcement. They realized that most of the people who got caught were petty criminals; harsh punishments were little deterrent for them, since many of them had no other means of survival. Neither were hardened criminals deterred by such punishments, for they stood little chance of actually being caught. The Methodist religion, founded in 1738 by John Wesley, who saw poverty as the root of much evil, was an important influence in the new thinking. So too was the French philosophy of *Enlightenment* which argued that it was wrong to run society by custom and to do things in certain ways simply because that was the way they had always been done. Men should think about how they lived, and work out the most rational way of doing things. The Englishman, Jeremy Bentham (1742-1832) had a similar idea which he called *Utilitarianism*. Society, he argued, should be organized to give the "greatest happiness to the greatest number". Punishment could only be justified if it could be proved to prevent worse evils. The key to law and order, therefore, might lie not in repression, but in eradicating poverty and increasing the likelihood that hardened criminals were caught.

THE FIELDING BROTHERS AT BOW STREET

In 1746 Henry Fielding was appointed Chief Magistrate (the name given to JPs in the towns) of Bow Street Magistrates' Court in London. He was a novelist and playwright – the author of *Tom Jones* – and an exponent of the new, enlightened thinking. He helped found a home for children who had been abandoned and who often grew up on the streets into a life of crime, and he was an opponent of the custom of imprisoning young prostitutes, whom he saw as victims rather than criminals.

What Fielding could do to change the society of his time was obviously limited, but he was in a position to do something about the large number of notorious criminals who regularly escaped justice. In 1750 he recruited six householders from the Bow Street district, who agreed to serve as constables beyond the usual term of one year. They wore no uniform but were paid a guinea a week, which Fielding found out of his own pocket. They were also allowed to keep any rewards they earned from private individuals. This small band of full-time constables were nicknamed "Mr Fielding's People" and had some spectacular successes in breaking up a number of notorious gangs of thieves. Henry Fielding died in 1754, before the work was barely underway, and was succeeded as magistrate by his blind half-brother, John, who continued and expanded the new force. In time they became known as the *Bow Street Runners*. In 1759 Fielding petitioned the government for a grant to help with his running expenses. He was so persuasive that he was given an annual sum of £400, the first official payment towards police expenses in English history.

A drawing of one of the early Bow Street Runners. What do you notice about the way he is dressed?

Advertisement by the Bow Street Runners:

TO THE PUBLIC

All Persons who shall for the future suffer Robbers, Burglars, &c. are desired immediately to bring or send the best description they can of such Robbers, &c. with the Time and Place, and Circumstances of the Fact, to Henry Fielding, Esq. at his House in Bow Street. And if they would send a special messenger on these occasions, Mr Fielding . . . would immediately dispatch A Set of brave Fellows in pursuit, who have long been engaged for such purposes, and are always ready to set out to any Part of this Town or Kingdom, on a Quarter of an Hour's Notice.

(*Source:* advertisement by the Bow Street magistrates' office, 20 December 1754. From the archives of the Metropolitan Police, quoted in P. Pringle, *Hue and Cry*, Museum Press, 1955)

What was the main function of the Bow Street Runners?

The Bow Street Runners at work:

Waylaying a Highwayman at a Turnpike 5s
Pursuing a Highwayman near Hackney 17s 6d
Sitting up in a hospital with a Highwayman that was wounded
until fit to be examined £1 11s 6d
Pursuing and apprehending Jonathan Wigmore, Highwayman,
for attempting to rob the King of Poland's groom. £8 8s 0d
For pursuing Watts, a Housebreaker, to Bristol, for
horse-hire for 20 days. £3 10s 0d

(*Source:* Bow Street Office Accounts for 1755, the Metropolitan Archives, quoted in
Pringle)

The Bow Street publications:

Fielding had a number of regular news-sheets printed at Bow Street,
including *The Public Advertiser, The Weekly or Extraordinary Pursuit* and
The Quarterly Pursuit. These were distributed throughout London, and
copies of the last two were pinned up on church doors and in inns and other
public places.

We have now the pleasure to inform the public that on Saturday and
Sunday last were apprehended, by the persons employed by Mr Fielding
for such purposes, that gang of robbers who have lately infested the
streets of this town and the roads round it. The gang consists of three of
the most desperate fellows, and all old offenders. . . . All persons robbed
within four months should go to Bow Street on Monday next when the
prisoners will be examined.

(*Source: Public Advertiser*, 1 January 1771)

Offenders at large:

Elizabeth Austin, alias Williams, alias Robinson, a tall girl, flaxen hair,
cast in her eyes, broad-shouldered, has a scar under her chin, charged
with felony in Middlesex.
Benjamin Bird, a tall thin man, pale complexion, black hair ties, thick lips,
the nail of his fore-finger of his right hand is remarkably clumsy, comes
from Coventry, and is with several forgeries, the last at Liverpool.
John Godfrey, pretends to be a clergyman, middle-sized, thin-visaged,
smooth face, ruddy cheeks, his eyes inflamed, a large white wig, bandy-
legged, charged with fraud at Chichester.

(*Source: Quarterly Pursuit*, 22 September 1772)

*In what ways would the publication and distribution of these news-sheets
help in crime prevention in London?*

The Bow Street Runners had quite a number of spectacular successes in their early years. In 1775 they recovered gold and silver plate stolen from the house of John Conyers, MP for Essex, and captured the thieves – all within twenty-four hours.

EARLY POLICE FORCES

On the heels of the Bow Street success, other small, professional police forces were set up here and there between 1760 and 1829, to meet special needs. In 1800, a 60-strong River Police was formed to guard valuable cargoes on the River Thames. In 1792 an Act of Parliament created seven new magistrates' offices in London, each of which had six full-time constables who were paid 12 shillings a week and allowed to arrest on suspicion of crime, and not just after a crime had been committed. The Bow Street Horse Patrol was formed in 1805, to patrol the roads on the outskirts of London against highwaymen. They were the first police force to wear a uniform and were nicknamed "Robin Redbreasts" after their scarlet waistcoats. Each man was paid 5 shillings a night.

THE PROBLEM OF RIOTING

The new police forces, however, touched only the tip of the iceberg, even in London; while outside the capital the rest of the country was as badly policed as ever. Neither was there any effective way of stopping riots getting out of hand. In 1780, when anti-Catholic riots, stirred up by an eccentric nobleman, Lord George Gordon, broke out in London, the existing forces of law and order could not cope and the Bow Street Magistrates' Court itself was burnt to the ground. Troops had to be called in, but the sight of armed soldiers on the streets only enraged the rioters even more. It took six days to bring the situation under control. Seven hundred people died, and untold damage was done to property. A similar sequence of events took place in Edinburgh during the Porteous riots in 1736, which are described by Sir Walter Scott in his novel *The Heart of Midlothian*. Decent people were shocked by the bloodshed, and men of property were thoroughly alarmed. Surely, it was argued, when the matter was debated in Parliament, there must be a better way of stamping out riotous behaviour before it got out of hand.

THE CASE FOR A NATIONAL FORCE

In 1797, early on during the Napoleonic Wars between England and France, a London magistrate of Scottish birth campaigned for a thorough reform of the English policing system. Patrick Colquhoun, who was a friend of Bentham, was a great admirer of the French system of paid government agents, who had made Paris one of the safest cities in Europe. In *A Treatise on the Police of the Metropolis* (1797), he argued that detection and crowd-control were now such skilled jobs that they could only be done by professionals. He advocated a nation-wide police force under the control of the Home Secretary. Over the next thirty years, Colquhoun's ideas were often debated in Parliament and always rejected.

The case against a national police force:

It is difficult to reconcile an effective system of police with that perfect freedom of action and exemption from interference which are the great privileges and blessing of society in this country; and Your committee think that the forfeiture or curtailment of such advantages are too great a sacrifice for improvements in police, or facilities in detection of crime, however desirable in themselves if abstractly considered.

(*Source:* Report of Commons Committee of 1820)

On what grounds does the committee reject the idea of a national police force?

What other factors at the time might have counted against it?

SCOTLAND

After 1603, England and Scotland shared the same monarch and in 1707 the two countries were formally united. Many Scots, especially Highlanders, had not accepted the deposition of James II in 1688. They were known as *Jacobites* and supported James's son, the "Old Pretender", when he tried to claim the throne in 1715. The attempt was unsuccessful, but the Jacobite uprising had an important effect on the development of the Scottish police. In 1724 Scottish counties were ordered to levy local taxes, or *rates*, to pay for a police force "for the apprehending and prosecuting of criminals", meaning the Jacobites. Because of her political situation, therefore, Scotland had proper county police forces over a century before England did. Then at the end of the eighteenth century, three expanding Scottish cities with similar law and order problems to their English counterparts – Glasgow (1800), Edinburgh (1805) and Perth (1811) – set up their own full-time city forces, thus scoring a "first" for Scotland here as well.

THE POST-1815 CRISIS

The end of the Napoleonic Wars in 1815 brought economic slump to Britain, and this affected the poor in town and countryside. Protest erupted everywhere. In 1812 gangs known as *Luddites* went around smashing the new factory machinery that they blamed for putting them out of work. Societies sprang up to campaign for a reform of the political system, to make it more responsive to the needs of ordinary people. The government under Lord Liverpool was in a continuous state of panic. In the absence of a professional police force, it was almost impossible to anticipate and head off trouble before it got out of hand. Sometimes spies were employed to mingle with the local people and find out if trouble was brewing.

Payment to spies:

Mr C. and his agents	£71
Mr W. and his agents	122 – 11 – 3
L. F. and his agent B.	34 – 17 – 0
Postages and various expenses	6 – 1 – 0
	234 – 9 – 3

(*Source:* Colonel Fletcher, a Bolton magistrate, to Henry Hobhouse, Under-secretary of State for Home Affairs, 30 April 1819)

Unreliable spies:

Mr Peel has desired me to send you in strict confidence the enclosed papers containing accounts given by a person known to Colonel Fletcher of Bolton, by whom they have been transmitted to me. The man has Mr Fletcher's confidence, but the internal evidence leads Mr Peel to suspect that the narrative, if not fabricated . . . is greatly exaggerated. He therefore wishes that you would consider them attentively and return them with your remarks, how far your evidence corroborates or negatives any of the facts stated, and your opinion on the whole matter. . .

(*Source:* letter from Henry Hobhouse to J.F. Foster, a Manchester magistrate, 21 July 1826)

Why is the employment of spies an unreliable means of keeping public order?

The alternative was repression. Between 1815 and 1820 the Habeas Corpus Act, which made it illegal to imprison people without trial, was suspended and public meetings of more than three people were banned. Events reached a climax in the summer of 1819, when a crowd of 60,000 people met in St Peter's Fields outside Manchester to listen to a famous orator, Henry Hunt, speak in favour of parliamentary reform. Armed soldiers were ordered by local magistrates to arrest Hunt. Instead, they panicked and ran amok in the crowd, killing eleven and injuring 400, of whom over 100 were women. As a result, the government became more unpopular than ever and unrest increased rather than diminished. The climate of opinion in Parliament began to change. The fear that a police force would be a threat to the traditional liberties of Englishmen did not die, but was now outweighed by fear of anarchy.

A comic picture, painted in 1820, of revellers attacking a Charley in London. What light does this throw on the growing support for the idea of a trained police force? When did London get its first proper force?

THE METROPOLITAN POLICE

Sir Robert Peel, who became Home Secretary in 1822, shared these views. His father was a Lancashire cotton manufacturer, and as a wealthy man himself he had come to believe that property rights and the stability of the country could only be guaranteed if there was a proper police force. Police trained in riot-control could break up trouble before it got out of hand. More criminals, too, might be deterred from crime by a greater likelihood of being caught than were ever put off by harsh punishments. "I want to teach people," he wrote to the Prime Minister, the Duke of Wellington, in 1829, "that liberty does not consist in having your house robbed by organized gangs of thieves, and in leaving the principal streets of London in the nightly possession of drunken women and vagabonds".

Between 1822 and 1824 Peel reduced by more than a half the number of offences carrying the death penalty. In 1829, after a seven-year struggle, his *Bill for Improving the Police in and near the Metropolis* passed through Parliament and the Metropolitan Police were born. London was to have a single police force covering an area within a seven-mile radius of Charing Cross. All the existing police forces within that area, except the Bow Street Runners, who continued until 1839, were swept away. The new 3,000-strong force was headed by two commissioners, responsible to the Home Office. The first two were Colonel Charles Rowan, an ex-soldier, and Richard Mayne, a barrister. Headquarters was a part of Whitehall Palace called Scotland Yard. The Metropolitan area was divided into 17 districts, each under the supervision of a *superintendant*, who had under him a hierarchy of inspectors, sergeants and constables. Policemen were to wear a uniform, which was deliberately designed to look as non-military as possible. Their powers of arrest were carefully limited and strict rules were laid down for their behaviour.

An 1830 drawing of a Peeler. The frock-coat was dark blue and the top hat reinforced with a metal frame to protect the head. On his right-hand side his truncheon or baton is seen protruding. What other piece of equipment would he have had, which cannot be seen here? In what way is his appearance "non-military"?

Why do you think the new police force applied only to London? There is an obvious answer to this question which may not, however, be the full one. Try to think of several reasons, for very few historical events have one simple cause.

Police duties and powers:

And be it enacted, that it shall be lawful for any man belonging to the said police force, during the time of his being on duty, to apprehend all loose, idle and disorderly persons whom he shall find disturbing the public peace, or whom he shall have just cause to suspect of any evil designs, and all persons whom he shall find between sunset and the hour of eight in the forenoon lying in any highway, yard, or any other place, or loitering therein, and not giving a satisfactory account of themselves, and to deliver any person so apprehended into the custody of the constable appointed under this act, who shall be in attendance at the nearest watch-house in order that such a person may be secured until he can be brought before a justice of the peace, to be dealt with according to the law.

(*Source:* Metropolitan Police Act, section 7)

What is the main job of a Metropolitan constable? How did it differ from that of a Bow Street Runner?

Instructions to policemen:

June 3, 1830. The commissioners . . . expressly state that the police constable is not authorised to take anyone into custody without being able to prove some specific act by which the law has been broken. No constable is justified in depriving anyone of his liberty for words only, and language, however violent, towards the police constable himself, is not to be noticed. . .

August 21, 1830. The constables are to recollect upon all occasions that they are required to execute their duty with good temper and discretion; any instance of unnecessary violence by them, in striking a party in their charge, will be severely punished. . .

September 31, 1830. The commissioners take the occasion to warn the whole of the Police force on the subject of the most perfect civility at all times being shown to the public, of whatsoever class, as any man who acts otherwise cannot be allowed to stay in the force.

(*Source:* General instructions for Constables, issued by the Metropolitan Police Commissioners, 1830)

In spite of Peel's care to make the new police force appear as part of the community, it was very unpopular at first among ordinary Londoners, especially when it was ordered to break up demonstrations. The police were nicknamed "Peel's Bloody Gang" or "Raw Lobsters" and they were often attacked. In time, the hostility abated. The crime rate dropped in London. As the police gained more experience in crowd-control by using baton charges or linked arms, their methods were compared favourably with the more brutal ones of the army. The turning point came in 1848, when a mass Chartist demonstration in favour of "one man, one vote" passed off peacefully and with good humour on both sides. Troops standing by in case of trouble were not needed.

IRELAND

Ireland had been ruled by England since the sixteenth century. The English were regarded by many Irishmen as oppressors, and unrest was common. In 1814, Peel, who was then Chief Secretary for Ireland, set up the Royal Irish Constabulary to maintain order. They were full-time, professional policemen, wore military-style uniforms, lived in barracks and were armed. They soon gained a reputation for efficiency but were often hated by the local population.

ON REFLECTION:

Do the differences between the organization of the Royal Irish Constabulary and the Metropolitan Police reflect the different circumstances in which they were created? If so, how? Does this also explain the difference in public reaction in the two countries?

Can you envisage any situations which might arise in nineteenth-century England that would cause the powers of the police to be increased? If so, what?

1830 – 1945

In the hundred years after 1830 Britain was transformed from a mainly rural nation into a largely urban one. At the same time a communications revolution took place, as the spread of railways in the 1840s was followed by the development of the telegraph and telephone and then, at the beginning of the twentieth century, by the radio and the motor car. Inevitably, these developments were accompanied by great social and political changes. It was against this background that Britain's first nation-wide system of professional police forces was born and developed its character.

During the second two-thirds of the nineteenth century the country as a whole prospered, and a large, comfortably-off middle class grew up. Parliamentary Reform Acts in 1832, 1867 and 1884 extended the right to vote, and political power passed from the landowning to the middle classes, who were less concerned with tradition than with the efficient running of the country, on which their wealth depended. The eighteenth-century prejudice against change disappeared, and there began a great era of reform in national life. Middle-class values, including belief in both the rights of the individual and the sanctity of private property, became predominant. All this did not happen without great social strain. Living and working conditions for the new urban workforce were often appalling. Dissatisfied workers formed trade unions to fight for better conditions and industrial conflict became increasingly common. Women became more resentful about their ages-old exclusion from political life.

A NATIONAL NETWORK OF POLICE FORCES

The formation of the Metropolitan Police had left unsolved the policing problems of the rest of the country. In 1835 the Municipal Corporations Act, which reformed local government, required every one of the new boroughs (towns large enough to have a mayor and corporation) to organize a paid police force under the supervision of a *watch committee* of local councillors. An act of 1839, which also extended the jurisdiction of the Metropolitan Police to a radius of 15 miles, permitted counties to set up forces of their own if they wished. Of the 56 counties in England and Wales, only 26 had done so by 1856. The main objections to doing so were the threat to local liberty and the cost to ratepayers.

This chaotic situation was finally resolved in 1856, when the County and Borough Police Act made it compulsory for each local authority to set up a full-time, professional police force headed by a Chief Constable and under the supervision of a *joint standing committee* of JPs and county councillors. (The head of the Metropolitan Police continued to be known as the *Commissioner.*) Each area was given wide powers to organize its own force as it thought fit, but *Inspectors of Constabulary* were appointed to tour the country and submit to the Home Secretary annual reports on the efficiency of each force. If the report was favourable, the local force would then receive a government grant towards the cost of pay and uniforms. In

1857 the act was extended to Scotland, so that the two countries' police forces have henceforth been organized on similar lines.

An act passed in 1831 gave all forces the right to swear in ordinary citizens as *special constables* in times of emergency. These powers were used by a number of cities, including London, at the time of the Chartist demonstrations in 1848.

Why was the decision to set up a nation-wide professional police system finally made in the 1850s?

To what extent was the English tradition of local control maintained?

RECRUITMENT

The main function of the new Victorian policeman was to deter crime by his presence, and when that failed, to pursue and catch the criminal. Few special qualifications were required. Most forces asked only that recruits be 5 feet 7 inches tall, able to read and write, and provide two character references. There was little formal training. Constables were expected to rely on common sense and an understanding of human nature, and to pick up the job as they went along. Pay was kept deliberately low – around the level of that earned by an unskilled labourer – so that only ordinary, working-class men, who were expected to understand the people among whom they worked, would be attracted to the job. Of the 3,179 policemen in the Metropolitan force in 1832, over half had formerly been unskilled labourers.

THE URBAN POLICEMAN

In the towns, each policeman was given a *beat*, small enough to be walked around. His job was to patrol that area throughout his shift. Most of the time he was on his own. If he ran into trouble which he could not handle, his only recourse was to shake his rattle (later these were replaced by whistles) and hope that help came, either from another constable nearby or from members of the public. Much of the work does not seem to have been very dramatic, but it was often tedious and uncomfortable, and sometimes dangerous. Often constables took over the watchman's old job of rousing people in the morning, and they were paid extra for this by their

An 1895 painting of a policeman on duty in the East End of London. Why is he blowing his whistle?

"customers". In London the going rate for this service was 6d a week. In some towns, such as Portsmouth, the police were also responsible for fighting fires. It was not until the 1930s that every area in the country had a separate fire brigade.

A London policeman's tally of arrests, 1857-73:

	Male	Female
Petty theft	21	3
Burglary	4 (including the arrest of one man on two separate occasions)	
Drunk and disorderly or drunk and incapable	15	12 (most of whom he describes as prostitutes)
Drunk in charge of a vehicle	20	—
Cab driver holding up traffic	18	—
Assault	5	—
Begging	2	1
Other	5	—
Not specified	1	1
	91	17

(*Source:* compiled from the notebooks of P.C. Alexander Hennessey, by Clive Emsley for his book, *Policing and its Context 1750-1870*, Macmillan, 1983)

A policeman remembers:

I found that the chief duty of a constable on beat was arresting drunks and escorting them to the station. Drunkenness was a major evil of the time, and it was impossible to walk about at night without meeting irresponsible revellers clinging to lamp-posts in a vain attempt to steady themselves. They seldom struggled and usually came quietly, save for an occasional hiccough.

My heart cried out for bigger things, and after a short spell on beat, I came to the conclusion that the sooner I could find a job with more prospects the better.

(*Source: From Vine Street to Jerusalem*, the memoirs of Joseph E. Broadbent, a London detective 1899-1932, published by Stanley Paul, 1936)

Instructions to a Manchester probationer;

"You check the time carefully", advised the sergeant, "and make sure you're not late at the meeting place. You pull every padlock and try the door latch. You walk this side one night and that side the next. Sometimes you go half way up one side and cross over and go half way up the other, doing it the opposite way round on the way back, see? You listen and report anything suspicious, anything at all, and you be careful if somebody asks you to step up to a drunk man or a sick woman. Keep your truncheon so that you can pull it. Think to get your back to the wall if you're threatened. If you can't get your truncheon out remember your helmet is just as good for belting them with".

(*Source:* The memories of P.C. Arthur Howells Williams of his probationary service in Manchester, circa 1900, published in Ian Niall, *The Village Policeman*, 1971)

THE RURAL POLICEMAN

Country policemen were assigned to a village, or group of villages, and took total responsibility for keeping law and order there around the clock. They were expected to live in the village and usually a special police house was provided for them. Although rural policing was not without its hazards, much of the time was spent dealing with the minor crime endemic in country areas, and the constable was often called upon to carry out jobs over and beyond the strict line of duty.

A rural police sergeant and his family in the garden of the police house at Beckley in East Sussex, c. 1893. This family looks well-fed and clothed, but the life of a policeman's wife was usually quite hard. In what ways, do you think?

Six days in the life of an East Sussex policeman:

That afternoon he is on duty again at 4pm until 8am on 30th, still watching for the thief. The last day of the year 1840 Sheather spends from 1am to 6pm, at first watching for his quarry, and later being in Battle from 10am to 3pm.

"to meet Thomas an Steven turnner then before the Magistrates Wen commted for Trial".

–He logs 27 miles.

On New Year's day 1841 he spends 8am to 8pm
"Moven wagrunce [vagrants] out of my district" (18 miles)
On 2nd January from 8am to 3am on the 3rd, he continues his watch for
"gorge Turner" and similarly from 5pm on the 3rd to 2am on the 4th.
After four hours' rest he books on at 5am to

"Lewes for witness gants [against] thomas and steven turnnere For
sheepsteling Steven turnner was found gilty and his sintance to
transported for ten years."

(*Source:* summary of the notebook of Constable Sheather of the East Sussex Police for the 29th December 1840 to 4th January 1841, quoted in *A History of the East Sussex Police 1840-1967*, R.V. Kyrke, 1969)

What can we learn about P.C. Sheather's educational background? What other qualities might he have had for the job?

Beyond the call of duty:

He was officer in charge, a sort of headman in the village, and in all cases of disputation the villagers came to him. They brought him more than their complaints. They brought him their fears, told him of a wayward son or daughter, a drunken husband, the furtive behaviour of a neighbour.

(*Source:* P.C. Williams' experience in the Welsh village of Tanygrisau, circa 1913, published in Ian Niall, *The Village Policeman*, 1971)

THE POLICEMAN'S LOT

In town and country, police work was seen as a public service rather than just an ordinary job. Constables were expected to put in as many hours as necessary, and the day was often gruellingly long. There was no right to a weekly rest day, and seven-day working weeks were common, with only a week's unpaid holiday each year. Pay remained low and there was no automatic pension entitlement. They were forbidden to form a union. Policemen and their families were expected to set an example to the community and there were numerous restrictions on their private life. They were, for instance, forced to attend church in uniform. In 1855, constables of the Metropolitan D Division complained to the Home Secretary that they were treated like "schoolboys".

Constables complain about pay:

Men joining the police service as 3rd class constables and having a wife and three children to support on joining, are not able properly to do so on the pay of 16/8d. Most of the married men are somewhat in debt, and are unable to extricate themselves on account of rent to pay and articles to buy which are necessary for support of wife and children.

(*Source:* petition presented by a group of Metropolitan constables to the Home Secretary, November 1848, quoted in *Policing and its Context*, C. Emsley, Macmillan, 1983)

Would conditions have been much different in rural areas? If not, what evidence can you bring to prove this?

Around the turn of the century some changes did take place in the policeman's lot, although unions were still forbidden. The 1890 Police Act granted every policeman the right to a pension after 25 years' service or, on medical grounds, after 15. In 1900 a weekly rest day was made compulsory. Some early technological developments made the job a little easier. Other than this, however, the life and working conditions of the average policeman changed little between the middle of the nineteenth century and the First World War.

New equipment:

Chief Constable's Office,
Lewes.
1st August 1895

I wish to inspect the Uckfield bicycle at Haywards Heath Police station on Monday next at 10.30 a.m.
Let the constable who usually has charge of it ride it to Haywards Heath in readiness for my inspection at the time named.

(*Source:* letter from the Chief Constable of the East Sussex Police to the Uckfield station, quoted in *A History of the East Sussex Police 1840-1967*, R.V. Kyrke, 1969)

For the construction of an enclosed place for the
reception and dispatch of telephone messages at the
Chief Constable's office   £7. 9. 0d.

(*Source:* accounts of the Standing Joint Committee of East Sussex, 19 October, 1896, quoted in *A History of the East Sussex Police 1840-1967*, R.V. Kyrke, 1969)

How might the bicycle and the telephone equipment help to make a policeman's job easier?

Policemen from Easebourne in West Sussex on "chicken and hen" bicycles in 1880. By this time all forces had replaced the top hat by a helmet (also reinforced) and the frock-coat with a tunic. Have police uniforms changed much since then?

THE PUBLIC IMAGE OF THE POLICE

The amount of petty crime and violence did decrease during the nineteenth century, and most people came to see the police as a useful and necessary part of society. Many rural policemen, in particular, became valued members of their community. Low pay, however, tended to attract mostly unskilled, poorly educated entrants, who were unlikely to qualify for better jobs elsewhere, and the public image of the average constable was of a worthy but rather thick "Mr Plod", who was good at breaking up fights and bringing in drunks but not much use at dealing with more sophisticated types of crime. There was also a suspicion that such poorly paid men could not be expected to be entirely honest or conscientious. Middle-class magazines like *Punch* enjoyed painting comic pictures of the police, while a popular song from the 1880 Gilbert and Sullivan opera *The Pirates of Penzance* complained that "A policeman's lot is not a happy one".

A cartoon appearing in the Comic Almanack in 1847. What image of the police is being shown here?

WHERE CAN THE POLICE BE?

THE DETECTIVE BRANCH

It soon became apparent that uniformed policemen were not very effective at solving serious crimes once they had been committed. In 1842 two Metropolitan constables, tracking down some stolen goods, went to interview a certain Daniel Good at his lodgings. There, purely by chance, they found the body of his wife, whom he had murdered. He managed to give them the slip and the police, although they knew just what he looked like, made such a mess of following his trail that he was not caught until nearly six months later, working as a bricklayer in Tonbridge, Kent. After that the "Met" set up a plain clothes squad of two inspectors and six sergeants. Their jurisdiction was limited to London, although they were sometimes invited to help local forces solve particularly baffling crimes. In 1865 the number of detectives was raised to fifteen.

The detective's job:

Tricks and contrivances of those who wheedle money out of you rather than steal it; who cheat you with your eyes open . . . for the detection and punishment of such imposters a superior order of Police is requisite, whose duty is to wear no uniform and to perform the most difficult operations of the craft. They have not only to counteract the machinations of every sort of rascal . . . but to clear up family mysteries, the investigation of which demands the utmost delicacy and tact. Sometimes they are called upon to investigate robberies, so executed that no human ingenuity appears to be capable of finding the thief. He leaves no trail or trace. Every clue seems cut off; but the experience of a detective leads him into tracks quite invisible to other eyes.

(*Source: Household Words*, a family magazine edited by Charles Dickens, 13 November 1844)

Why do you think that the ordinary police were of little use in solving this sort of crime?

The detective branch had some early successes but also some spectacular failures. *Punch* labelled it the "Defective Department". In 1867 a bomb planted by a group of Irish nationalists called the Fenians exploded at Clerkenwell in London, killing a number of women and children who were passing by. Queen Victoria herself criticized the failure of the Metropolitan Police to uncover the plot in advance. As a result, a new corps of 80 detectives was set up, which in 1878 was renamed the *Criminal Investigation Department* or *CID*. Members, who were recruited from among serving policemen, were then seconded to individual police stations throughout London to work alongside the uniformed branch. Often there was friction, as detectives were better-paid and enjoyed superior status. The *Special Branch* was also set up at the same time, specifically to deal with terrorist attacks. It still exists today.

The reputation of the CID was mixed at first. In 1880 a French lady living in Park Lane in London was murdered by her Belgian maid, who then stole all her money. The CID men put on the case were baffled at first by being given three different descriptions of the wanted woman, but soon worked out that this might be because she was fond of buying lots of clothes and dressing up in different styles. Maybe that was why she needed the money! Detectives were sent to a number of big European cities to call at all the stores and ask about a lady who was fond of buying finery. Before long, she was arrested in Paris. In 1881, by a similar combination of ingenuity and hard work, the CID solved a gruesome murder on the London to Brighton train. These cases and others won them a great deal of praise at home and abroad, but they were also bitterly criticized for their failure to catch a notorious killer known as Jack the Ripper, who murdered eight women in London's East End in 1888 and 1889. The Sherlock Holmes stories by Sir Arthur Conan Doyle illustrate the low opinion many people had of professional detectives at this time. *Punch* often poked fun at them.

In solving crimes the nineteenth-century detective was dependent on eye-witnesses, informers and any clear clues that criminals might leave behind. However, all this changed after 1903, when Sir Edward Henry became Commissioner of the Metropolitan Police. In his previous job as Inspector-General of Police in Bengal, he had been intrigued by the way Indians used the impress of the thumb and fingers as a signature, and he had gone on to work out how this knowledge might help police work. He discovered that not only is each human fingerprint almost unique (we now know that the chance of two people having identical prints is more than 1

IN THE SCOTLAND YARD ARCHIVES: A FINGER-PRINT REGISTRATION-FORM.

PHOTOGRAPHS SPECIALLY TAKEN FOR "THE ILLUSTRATED LONDON NEWS" BY SCOTLAND YARD.

H.C.R. No. _____

Name _____
Aliases _____
Prison _____
Prison Reg. No. _____

This Form is not to be pinned.

MALE.

Classification No. 25. [0.1.] 15
9. [1.1.]

RIGHT HAND.

1.—Right Thumb.	2.—R. Fore Finger.	3.—R. Middle Finger.	4.—R. Ring Finger.	5.—R. Little Finger.
(Fold.) LOOP.	WHORL.	WHORL.	WHORL.	(Fold.) LOOP.

Impressions to be so taken that the flexure of the last joint shall be immediately above the black line marked (Fold). If the impression of any digit be defective a second print may be taken in the vacant space above it.

When a finger is missing or so injured that the impression cannot be obtained, or is deformed and yields a bad print, the fact should be noted under *Remarks*.

LEFT HAND.

6.—L. Thumb.	7.—L. Fore Finger.	8.—L. Middle Finger.	9.—L. Ring Finger.	10.—L. Little Finger.
(Fold.) ARCH.	LOOP.	LOOP.	LOOP.	(Fold.) LOOP.

LEFT HAND.	**RIGHT HAND.**
Plain impressions of the four fingers taken simultaneously.	Plain impressions of the four fingers taken simultaneously.

Impressions taken by _____ Rank _____ Prison _____
Governor's Signature _____ Date _____
Classified at H.C. Registry by _____ Date _____
Tested at H.C. Registry by _____ Date _____

P.T.O.

ONE OF MANY THOUSAND FORMS: THE METHOD BY WHICH THE FINGER-PRINTS OF CRIMINALS ARE PRESERVED.

(continued)
A champagne-bottle bears two finger-prints left by a burglar after entering a house in Birmingham. In this case an officer of the Birmingham City Police took to New Scotland Yard the bottle referred to, and within a few minutes typical prints were found in the finger-print records. The accused was arrested the same day. It has been found that, when a finger comes in contact with a cold, dry, smooth surface, the pattern of the ridges is left more or less distinct on the article touched. They have been found on plated goods, window-panes, glasses, bottles, painted wood, and even on candles. The impression on the candle shown was left by a burglar, and was the clue which led to his arrest. The tumbler bears the finger-impressions of a notable criminal. The glass was found in a house he entered in a West End square. The thief helped himself to a glass of wine, and in this action left an indisputable clue, which resulted in his arrest and sentence to four years' penal servitude. Of particular interest is the calendar. This was the first case in which finger-print evidence of identification was adduced in court and accepted. The calendar bears a thumb-impression in blood, and was left by the criminal who murdered a tea-planter, in 1898, in the Julpaiguri district of Bengal. The system was not adopted by Scotland Yard until July 1901, since which time it has resulted in some **44,000** identifications being made, and, so far as is known, without error. The finger-impressions of two anthropoid apes—a chimpanzee and an orang-outang—are given for comparison with those of human beings. These were taken at the London Zoological Gardens, and it is only fair to add, perhaps, that they were not made because of any criminal tendencies on the part of the apes, but purely in the interests of science.

A copy of a finger-print registration form published in The Illustrated London News *in 1910. Why is so much care taken to record the details of every finger?*

in 64,000,000,000), but that anyone who touches a hard surface leaves drops of sweat which make a pattern of his or her print. When the area is dusted with fine powder, the print can be seen clearly through a magnifying glass. Henry brought his revolutionary idea to his new job, and in 1905 prints were used for the first time as vital evidence in a trial, at which Albert Stretton was convicted of robbing and murdering a shopkeeper and his wife. From that day on, fingerprints have been a vital tool of the detective. Each year between 1905 and 1914 about four times as many crimes were solved as had been solved in the year before.

Detective sections developed only slowly and haphazardly in the rest of the country. Even in the 1920s, many rural areas simply put a uniformed constable into plain clothes, if disguise was considered necessary, and left him to get on with solving the crime.

POLICEWOMEN

Before the First World War, suggestions that women might be employed as regular police officers had been scorned. In 1914, however, some women, many of whom had been suffragettes, volunteered to do police duties in place of policemen who had joined the armed services. Although some hard-pushed big-city forces accepted their services, only a few of the women were ever sworn in as full-time uniformed constables. Most had to remain as unpaid volunteers who were marked out only by a special arm-band and did not have the power of arrest. They were mainly assigned responsibilities seen as appropriate to women, such as protecting young girls in towns where there were army camps, or looking after the welfare of refugees and women munitions workers. As the manpower shortage grew more acute, however, the women were given a wider range of duties. London volunteer constables, for example, were responsible for patrolling tube stations.

Why should police forces have accepted the services of women in wartime?

Nina Boyle, founder of the Women's Volunteer Police, believed that her policewomen would aid the whole cause of women's emancipation. If they proved that they could do the job, it would boost their own self-esteem and make it difficult for men to go on saying that women were incapable of coping with demanding work.

A policewoman at work in London:

Another returning soldier was so disordered that while he was going down the stairs into the tube station, becoming suddenly aware of the crowds of people coming up, he looked haggardly about, and evidently mistaking the hollow space below for the trenches and the ascending crowd for Germans, fixed his bayonet and charged. But for the woman constable on duty at the turn of the staircase, who was quick enough to divine his trouble and hang on to him with all her strength to prevent his forward advance, he would have wounded many and caused danger and panic.

(*Source: The Pioneer Policewoman*, the memoirs of Mary Allen, Chatto and Windus, 1925)

A Metropolitan policewoman on duty in Trafalgar Square in 1921 (from The Illustrated London News, *5 February 1921). Does this picture tell us anything about the sort of work generally thought suitable for female constables? Do such ideas live on today?*

What does this extract show about women's ability to do police work? What effect would such incidents have had on women's self-esteem?

After the war the status of women in general improved. Women over 30 were given the vote and allowed to become MPs and sit on juries, but Nina Boyle's dream did not really come true. Although some full-time regular policewomen were recruited in the big cities for the first time, their numbers were small. So that there was no possibility of their ever being in a position to give orders to men, the women had to form a separate division within each force and be on a lower pay-scale. Most of their work was confined to "women's issues" and their early days on the force were far from easy. When cut-backs were made in times of economic depression they were the first to go. Portsmouth's two policewomen, for example, were asked to resign in 1922 when the force was cut from 308 to 290.

A policewoman remembers:

We twenty-five women were not unaware of the hostility we were to meet. We already had experience of what lay in store for us: but of the downright malice and vindictive spirit to be shown by some of the men towards us we were, as yet, blissfully ignorant.

(*Source: A Woman at Scotland Yard* by Lilian Wyles, who became a policewoman with the Metropolitan Police in 1920, Faber and Faber, 1952)

Why should male constables treat women police officers so?

POLICE STRIKE　Pay for most workers had risen dramatically during the war, when labour was short, but police pay had not. At the same time, the war had heaped extra duties on the police – from the enforcement of blackout regulations and new pub opening hours to dealing with the effects of Zeppelin raids on

Policemen on strike in 1919. How does the way these men are behaving differ from the usual way policemen stand to be photographed? Does this tell us anything about their mood?

east coast towns. By the end of the war frustrations were boiling over. An illegal trade union, the *Police Union*, brought 6,000 Metropolitan constables out on strike for twenty-four hours in August 1918. Further strikes took place in other cities in August 1919. In Liverpool over 200 striking policemen were sacked.

Alarmed, the government set up the Desborough Commission, to enquire into police pay and conditions of service. Policemen of all ranks gave evidence before the Commission.

The strikers' case:

In the past a policeman has been paid no more than an ordinary labourer; consequently he has been respected and regarded accordingly. He has been looked upon as one, who, for a tip or a free drink, could be made to neglect his duty. Unfortunately, his continual fight against poverty has only too often made him susceptible to bribes. There is no doubt we are now suffering from our lowly origin. There is no comparison between what is expected of a policeman today and the policeman of old. Our predecessors were invariably big, illiterate men, from whom little was expected. Nowadays a policeman must be as brave as a lion, as patient as Job, as wise as Solomon and as cunning as a fox . . . must be learned in criminal law, must be of strong moral character, a support to the weak, able to rise above all moral temptations, be prepared to act as a doctor and a terror to evil-doers, a friend and conciliator to all classes of the community and a walking encyclopaedia.

(*Source:* Testimony of Sergeant George Miles to the Desborough Commission 1919)

How does Sergeant Miles think the job has changed since the early days? How does his testimony help to explain why the police went on strike?

Why do you think the government listened to police complaints and gave such a generous settlement? That doesn't happen to most strikers, then or now.

At the end of the hearings the Commission granted an immediate 30% pay rise and a basic eight-hour day. Although the ban on trade unions remained, the *Police Federation* was set up to act as a spokesman for the rank and file, so that such a build-up of resentment should never happen again.

Most significant of all, however, was a change in the status and public image of the police. The strike had convinced the government that the morale of the police must be maintained at all costs. From that time onwards, police pay was usually pegged at a higher than average rate, and police work came to be seen as a respectable career. During the 1926 General Strike, in which the police played a key role in maintaining order and keeping essential services going, their prestige soared among the influential middle class. The image of the unflappable, ever-courteous "Bobby", who did his job with fairness and impartiality, dates from these years. The English often compared their police favourably with their armed foreign counterparts, who were more often feared than respected by the public.

CHANGES IN POLICING BETWEEN THE WARS

Between the wars further technological advances began to change the nature of police work. By 1939 there were over three million private cars on the roads and about one sixth of uniformed police officers were employed solely in directing traffic and enforcing motoring laws. Criminals, too, had become more mobile and difficult to catch. On the police side, a whole range of new scientific aids for the detection of crime were becoming available, from two-way radios to the detailed analysis of blood groups and hair types. If these were to be used to maximum advantage, the police would have to be specially trained and the old custom of learning the job as they went along modified. Some progress was made. In 1919 the *Flying Squad* was set up to deal with the growing number of smash-and-grab raids. Its detectives were fully mobile and could operate anywhere in the country, not just in their own areas. Big-city forces like Brighton and Nottingham experimented with two-way radios and radio-cars. Most forces acquired a few cars or motor cycles and trained some drivers. Centralized laboratories were set up, where expensive forensic techniques could be made available to small, local forces. But the vast majority of police officers went on doing the job just as it had been done for the past hundred years.

THE SECOND WORLD WAR

The Blitz and the vastly increased number of regulations governing civilian life put an even greater burden on the police than had been the case in the 1914-18 war. At the same time many constables volunteered to serve in the armed forces. To overcome the manpower shortage, 130,000 *special constables* were recruited from among men too old or unfit for active army service. They did their duties in addition to their normal job, were unpaid except for expenses, and wore no uniform except a special arm-band.

As a miner in the Welsh coalfields in the 1920s and 1930s my father had come to hate the way law and order was enforced during industrial disputes and to distrust uniforms of any kind. But he hated the Nazis so much that he was one of the first to volunteer in 1939. He was fifty four and much too old for the army, so he joined the Specials. His main job was guarding the large munitions works in Bridgend and sometimes he had to go round checking up that people were obeying the blackout. Most of the time it was boring rather than dangerous. – not like in the towns where the police had to deal with the effects of all the bombing – but he did have one narrow escape. His factory was bombed once but only one went off. This was lucky, as the naval shells being manufactured there could have blown up half the town.

(*Source:* Mrs Glenys Campling talking about her father, James Merriman, who was a wartime Special in Bridgend in South Wales)

Special constables and regular policemen sharing a recreation room. Which are which?

Why did James Merriman join the Special Constabulary?

What sort of duties did the Specials perform? Why could not these have been done by the regular police?

In what way is the idea of special constables in times of emergency part of an old British tradition?

The war also gave a boost to the recruitment of policewomen, whose numbers had been more or less static since the early 1920s. Some 400 extra full-time policewomen and 3,700 part-time auxiliaries were on duty by 1945 and many of them were kept on after the war. The bravery shown by many policewomen during the Blitz did much for their image amongst the public.

What effect did both world wars have on the role of policewomen?

Why do wars have this effect?

ON REFLECTION:

In what ways did the development of the police reflect the tradition that the police should remain as close to the community as possible?

How and why did the image of the police change between 1829 and 1945?

1945 to the Present Day

The pace of social change accelerated in Britain after 1945. There were great advances in living standards and education, from which all classes of the population benefited. Technological innovation changed the way people lived. Ownership of cars became widespread, and so too did international air travel. By the 1970s cheap microcomputers were bringing about an information revolution that is not yet at an end. While these changes brought benefits to many, they also brought new stresses to society. Contrary to expectations, the crime rate did not fall with increasing affluence but rose steadily. At the same time, criminals became more mobile and technologically sophisticated. Examples of this are the great train robbery of 1963 and the Brinks-Mat raid of 1983, when £24 million-worth of bullion was stolen from Heathrow Airport. More police manpower has had to be diverted into traffic duties. International air travel has been accompanied by the growth of international crimes such as drug smuggling and hijacking.

Many people believe that British society has become much more violent and anti-authoritarian, especially since the 1960s. The mounting level of violence is not confined, as might be expected, to areas of social deprivation, but is more widespread than that and expresses itself in a variety of ways from football hooliganism and unprovoked attacks on passing policemen and women to the growing number of criminals who carry and use firearms. In 1985 *The Times* reported that more police officers had been killed in the first five years of the 1980s than in any decade this century. The number of crimes of violence against the person reported to the police rose from 97,000 in 1980 to 125,000 in 1986. All these developments have affected the job, although there is only room here to look at a few of the problems they have raised.

Policemen dealing with crowd trouble at a football match at White Hart Lane in August 1986. Many policemen today feel that changes in society have made their job much more demanding and difficult. What effect has this had on recruitment and job satisfaction?

Everyone coming into the police force starts at the bottom as a uniformed constable on two years' probation. This time is divided between classroom training and learning the job on the streets. After the probationary period, police constables may carry on with ordinary uniformed police work or opt for one of the specialized sections such as the CID or the traffic police. Promotion is on merit. Police officers are still usually unarmed and each force is still independently run. During the miners' strike of 1984-5 police were sent from other districts to help forces in areas affected by the strike, but this could not be done without the invitation of the local Chief Constable. More and more of the money needed to run police forces, however, comes from central government, and this is giving the government increasing control over matters such as the number of men and women each force can employ. The Metropolitan Police still have a slightly special status. They publish the *Police Gazette*, which contains details of unsolved crimes (including descriptions of stolen goods) and send it free to forces around the country. On the invitation of a local Chief Constable, Metropolitan detectives are still occasionally sent to investigate serious crimes committed outside London.

According to the current police training manual, the main responsibility of the modern police officer is still "the protection of life, the prevention of crime and the maintenance of the peace". But the way in which this is done has changed dramatically since 1945. A shortage of recruits and government cut-backs have meant that many forces are chronically under strength. It has been estimated that every beat requires five regular constables, one to work each of the three shifts and two as back-up in case someone is absent because of illness or training courses. Many forces are too short-staffed to be able to manage this. A recent article in the *Chichester Observer* pointed out that the city has only four constables available to patrol the city round the clock. When the constable on duty makes an arrest, and has to take the suspect to the station, it can mean leaving the beat unmanned, sometimes for hours. Forces have had to look, therefore, for ways of using their people more efficiently. In many towns, beat constables have been replaced by car patrols, which can respond more quickly to emergencies and chase motorized criminals. All constables and cars are now equipped with two-way radios. Some large authorities like the West Midlands have a computer system that can tell where every officer and car is at any given moment and enable them to be deployed more effectively. During their probationary period, young constables have to spend more and more time learning to operate the new technology and less and less time in the streets. In the interests of cost effectiveness, the days of the village constable may also be numbered. Many serving policemen and women feel that in the emphasis on efficiency, some important values may have been lost.

Changes in police work in recent years: the comments of a Liverpool policeman, mid-1970s:

When I joined [8 years before], my beat at Birkenhead was as rough as any . . . and everyone knew me. I made an effort to know everyone, and you'd say "Well, So-and-so, what's yer lad doing tonight?" You'd laff and joke about it, and you'd be digestin' all the time. That is the way, in my opinion, to do police work.

But over here you've no longer got the bobbies on the streets because there're not enough policemen to do the job, or you're driving past situations and haven't the time to get involved. Y'know, you haven't the time to go round and visit Mrs Jones, who lives on her own and has to carry her coal up to her top flat every day. You should have the time, because that's as much part of police work as going out arresting thieves.

(*Source:* testimony of a panda car driver from A division of the Merseyside police, quoted in James McClure, *Spike Island. Portrait of a Police Division,* Macmillan, 1980)

The comments of a Sussex policeman, 1988:

There's no doubt we're far more efficient at answering emergency calls than we used to be in the old days, now we've got cars and radios, but the public still like to see policemen on the street, helping people and answering queries. At the same time, they want us to be there quickly to answer those 999 calls. There's a contradiction. There was an experiment once with putting *all* our policemen into cars and it was a dismal failure. At a stroke the close contact between the police and public was destroyed. So now we try to strike the best balance we can. We have some men on foot, but we also have to keep some back to respond to calls.

(*Source:* Chief Inspector Bond of the Bognor Regis Division of the Sussex Police in an interview with the author, April 1988)

These two policemen work in very different areas – one in a deprived inner city, the other in an affluent town on the south coast – but they have both experienced the same changes in policing methods. How are these likely to have affected their relations with the local community and the effectiveness with which they do their work? Would you expect the reaction to be different in each area?

How might changes in policing methods have affected the police's own morale and job satisfaction?

In recent years it has been suggested that some of the hostility towards the police, especially in inner-city areas, is due to the growing remoteness of the police from the community. After the Brixton riots of 1981 forces throughout the country were advised to set up *Community and Police Panels* to foster closer links between police and public. Many urban forces are doing their best to revive the custom of having a regular constable on the beat who was a familiar part of the local community.

The emphasis on efficiency has strengthened the case for establishing a national police force under central direction. This has not happened yet, but in 1966 and 1974 many of the smaller forces were amalgamated with neighbouring ones, so that there are now fewer and larger local forces – 43, in all, in England and Wales. The East Sussex force mentioned in chapter 5 has now been amalgamated with the West Sussex force and with those from towns like Brighton, Chichester and Hastings, to form the Sussex

The modern image of the police, taken on Brighton seafront in the early 1980s. What does this tell us about the way police work has changed since the Second World War?

Police . Central record banks have been set up to provide a common pool of information. In 1974 the police national computer was opened in Hendon in North London, and this provided local forces with instant access to criminal records. Its first facility was a record of stolen vehicles and their owners, from all over the country. The CID have added other specialized teams like the Regional Crimes squads and the Fraud squad.

In what way might these developments help to make the police more efficient?

What drawbacks might they have?

THE TV IMAGE OF THE POLICE

In our age, television and films provide a useful yardstick for looking at the public image of the police. A 1950 film, *The Blue Lamp*, and the television series *Dixon of Dock Green* that followed it, showed the life of a London constable, who was as much a father-figure to the community as a law-enforcer. Since the 1960s, however, beginning with series like *Z-Cars* and *Softly, Softly*, the TV image of the police has tended to become tougher and more professional, but at the same time less friendly and reassuring.

How are the English police depicted in TV fiction today?

THE POLICE AND SOCIAL TENSION

Social tensions in Britain have run particularly high in the 1970s and '80s. Although many people are still affluent, unemployment has risen to over three million and there are many, especially in the declining industrial regions of the Midlands and North or in the derelict inner-city areas, who feel that society has little to offer them. Against this background the police have suffered much public criticism over their handling of certain incidents and their image has taken a battering. In 1981 and 1985 serious rioting broke out among the black communities in cities like Bristol and Liverpool and in parts of London. Rioters blamed the police, claiming that black youths had been the victims of racialist attitudes among local constables and had been unfairly harassed. During the 1984-5 miners' strike, the police were accused of taking the side of the government and employers and of using undue brutality against pickets. Among many young people, especially in areas of high unemployment and deprivation, the image of the police is a highly negative one. In a survey conducted by *The Times* in January 1984, 42% of under-21s interviewed thought that the police were "not on their side". Whatever the truth of individual allegations, many policemen and women feel that overall public reaction has been grossly unfair.

We are the visible presence left at the end of the day. The identifiable target. I can't imagine they will have a riot at the housing office or the education office, but they will have a go at the police which is the culmination of all their problems.

(*Source:* a comment by Inspector Alderson of the Merseyside Police, published in *The Times*, 1 October 1985)

Who does Inspector Alderson mean by "they"?

What was the Inspector trying to say here?

THE PROBLEM OF STRESS

This feeling that they are being made the scapegoat for social problems not of their own making may be one reason for the high drop-out rate among both young and experienced constables, in spite of relatively high pay, fringe benefits and good career prospects. There are a number of other reasons as well.

Policemen speak about stress:

The uniform used to be some protection, but now it's "Why not give the old Bill a smack while we're at it?" The stress builds up. Your bottle goes. Mine went.

After a while it became impossible to wind down. I was pushed down the stairs in a pub. I went off sick eight months ago and I've never been back.

(*Source:* statement by Sergeant Y of the Metropolitan Police, in *Stress: a force to be reckoned with*, an article in the *TV Times*, 9-15 January 1988)

It isn't just that we are more aware of it. It's got a lot worse in recent years. The workload goes up all the time, especially as there are fewer police in proportion to the population than ever before. We seem sometimes to be giving a fire brigade service, rushing from call to call and never having time to do anything properly. Young policemen in particular, although it affects older ones too, can get swamped, especially by the paperwork. They have to write up this accident report but in the middle they're called out because an alarm goes off somewhere or a report of a fight starting comes in. The second thing is the increased likelihood of assault. We had this young lady who was with us for a year and then left. One of the reasons – it wasn't the main one – was that she had been assaulted twice in that year.

(*Source:*Chief Inspector Bond, Bognor Regis Division of the Sussex Police, interviewed April 1988)

Do you think police work has always been stressful? If so, in what ways?

What factors have made it worse in recent years and what effect might this have on recruitment?

DETECTION Dramatic advances in forensic techniques have made it possible now for detectives to solve crimes that would have been insoluble even a few decades ago. Lasers show up fingerprints on wood and fabric (where they were previously invisible) and can even trace where someone stood on a carpet many hours before. A machine called a spectrometer can find and analyse the minutest traces of hair, blood, glass or paint left on clothing, that would be invisible even under a microscope. From the results, detectives can discover things like the make, model and year of the car from which the paint chips came. In other ways, though, the detective's job is still similar to that of his nineteenth-century predecessor.

A detective today:

Let's face it. Ninety per cent of a detective's "deductions" are the result of sheer hard slog, just like they always were. All right, we have the sciences. The fingerprint and forensic people for the bad jobs like rapes and murders, where you collect and collate the evidence like hairs and that. And some crimes get solved that way that would never be solved otherwise, so I'm not knocking the scientific stuff at all. But with the average burglar, apart from prints, you don't usually have this. You have to spend a lot of time just going from door to door asking questions and just sitting watching places. It can get very boring. A lot of it is keeping

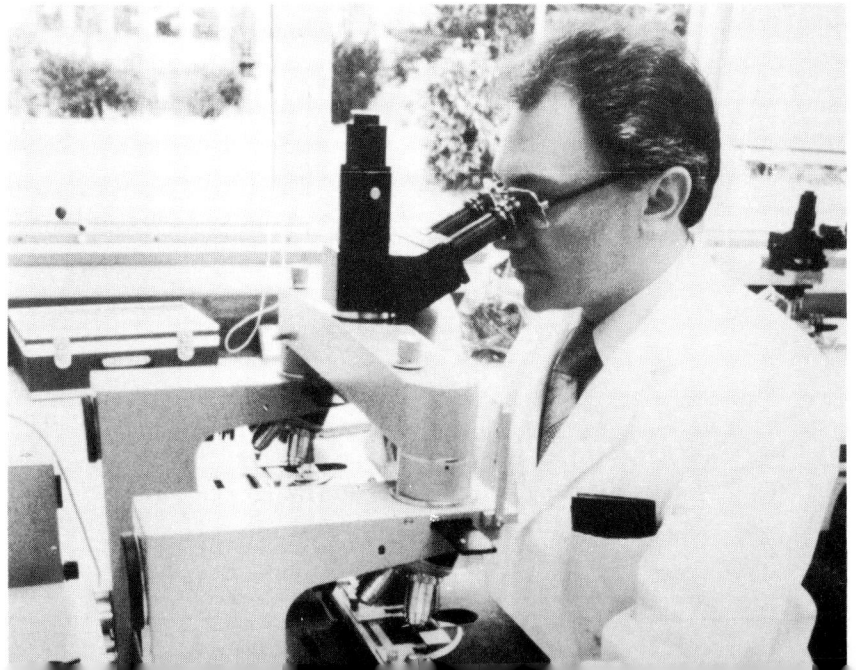

A forensic scientist at work. What might he be looking at? What sort of crimes are modern forensic techniques most useful in solving?

your ears open for snippets of information, and of course you need to have your informers. You wouldn't get far without them.

(*Source:* Detective Sergeant from Merseyside A Division, speaking to James McClure in *Spike Island. Portrait of a Police Division*, Macmillan, 1980)

A Punch *cartoon from 1950, when policewomen were becoming more numerous. What does it tell us about public attitudes towards policewomen? Do you think attitudes are different today?*

POLICEWOMEN

Policewomen have now become an established part of all police forces. The 1970 Equal Opportunities Act means that they now receive the same pay as men and discrimination against them in the type of work they are allowed to do is illegal. In 1984 Jenny Hill became the first female commander in the Metropolitan Police, and there is even a TV series, *Juliet Bravo*, about a woman inspector in charge of a small urban station. However, policewomen still form only about 10% of the total force (about 6% in Scotland) and have their own special problems.

A modern policewoman speaks:

Quite a few of the lads won't work with a policewoman. They think they're a liability. But a lot of the lads are good about it. They see for themselves if you're good. . . . But I do feel the onus is on me to prove myself and you do get a bit fed up with it after a while. Especially when young lads come along and assume because you're a woman you're no good, but you know you could run rings round them.

(*Source:* WPC Janice Rodgers of the Metropolitan Police in an interview with Sally Brompton in *The Times*, 5 June 1987)

Do you think a woman going into the police force might find it more difficult to be accepted as an equal there than in other professions? If so, why?

Can you suggest ways in which (a) the education system and (b) police training might be used to help improve attitudes towards policewomen in the future?

NORTHERN IRELAND

In 1922 the Republic of Ireland or Eire was created, leaving only Northern Ireland or Ulster as part of Britain. The Royal Irish Constabulary became the Royal Ulster Constabulary. Because of the tensions between Catholic and Protestant communities there, the RUC remained armed and was feared and distrusted by the Catholic minority. In 1969, at the beginning of the troubles that have lasted to the present day, a royal commission decided that the RUC itself was an important cause of tension and disarmed it. The army took over its riot-control duties and the RUC became more like its English and Scottish counterparts. Even today, however, few Catholics trust the Ulster police.

THE SATISFACTION OF THE JOB

A policeman remembers:

I joined in 1956, so I've been in the service over thirty years. Would I become a policeman if I had my time over again? The answer's not as straightforward as you might think. On balance, for myself, the answer is "yes". But knowing what I know now about the pressures that have arisen in recent years, it does raise doubts. It is interesting to note that some colleagues, who are nearing retirement, are quite sure that they wouldn't, knowing what they know now.

Overall, though, I've got real satisfaction from the job and feel that I've spent my life serving the community, which is what the job is really all about. There is great satisfaction, you know, when, for example, we go to a traffic accident where some poor fellow has been hit by another car. It wasn't his fault at all. The other driver was on the wrong side of the road or drunk, and you are able to sort things out for him and get him out of his difficulties – arrange for him to be put up for the night, look after his car – that sort of thing. And another good thing is the variety. You never know from one moment to another what is going to happen. And, you know, most young policemen and women today still join for the same reasons. They get on well with people and like to help them. You'd be surprised at how many of them do things in their spare time to help people – Scouts, St John's Ambulance, Mencap – all sorts of things. It's all part of the same motive that made them join the force. It would be very wrong to see the police only in a negative light, which so many do nowadays.

(*Source:* Chief Inspector Bond, Bognor Regis Division of the Sussex Police, interviewed April 1988)

ON REFLECTION:

What are likely to be the greatest problems faced by the police in their relations with the community in the near future?

Can you suggest any measures that the police themselves might take to improve the situation?

Do you see police work as an attractive career for a young person nowadays? If not, why not?

Glossary

abettor	someone who helps another in a crime
abjure	to swear an oath to give up or leave
affray	street fight or riot
apprehend	to arrest
bill	bill-hook or pike, carried by sixteenth- and seventeenth-century watchmen
carriage	behaviour, the overall way that a person conducts himself or herself
chastise	to scold or punish
conciliator	someone who settles arguments peacefully
deprecated	scorned or belittled
deter	to put off
disputation	argument
ell	an Anglo-Saxon measurement of length equivalent to about 45 inches (104 cm)
endemic	always present
fabricate	to make up
felon	someone who has committed a serious crime or *felony*
fence	someone who receives stolen goods and disposes of them for profit
forensic	scientific investigation of clues left on the scene of a crime
guile	cunning
Habeas Corpus	a law first passed in 1679 which made it illegal to hold suspects in custody without bringing charges against them. This meant that a person could not be kept in prison for a long time without a trial. The law is still in force in Britain today.
harness	equipment or arms
homicide	illegal killing, murder
incumbent	involving someone in a duty or obligation
knave	rascal
lucrative	likely to bring in lots of money
machinations	plots usually with evil intentions
mass-priest	priest of the Catholic Church who has authority to give Holy Communion
miscreant	wrong-doer, villain
mutilation	deliberate injury or disfigurement
Old Bill	slang term for the police, used mainly in London
prentice	apprentice or young man who is learning a trade under a skilled craftsman
presentment	the accounts given to the Assizes by local constables of the crimes committed in their neighbourhood and of the action taken
profane	treat or talk of sacred things without due respect; often used to describe use of God's name as a swear word
purlieu	the area lying round about
requisite	that which is necessary to achieve something
semi-literate	barely able to read or write
smite	hit
sojourner	someone who stays somewhere
strive	fight
suffragette	a campaigner for votes for women in early twentieth-century England
township	unit of local government in sixteenth- and seventeenth-century England. It might comprise one large or several small villages
unappeasable	cannot be made good or forgiven
zealous	enthusiastic, almost to an excessive degree
Zeppelin	German airship of First World War era

Sources

a review of the types of evidence and sources used in this book

Autobiographical writings
Very few of these were published until this century. Mary Allen and Lilian Wyles, two early policewomen, have told their story. (See the Book List.)

Diaries
The diary of PC Williams, which was written up in book form by Ian Niall, is one of the few intimate accounts of the daily life of an ordinary constable in the early twentieth century.

Films and television
Fictional dramas about the police give an insight into public images of the police. Many serving policemen, however, find them totally unrealistic.

Historical texts
Because law and order is so fundamental to all societies, many clues about policing can be gleaned from the works of contemporary writers like Tacitus or the Anglo-Saxon chroniclers.

Legal records
Records of Quarter Sessions and Assizes, which go back in some parts of England to the Middle Ages, provide much valuable information about the work of the police, including the annual presentments. They can often be found in the County Archive. However, West Sussex, where the author lives, destroyed the pre-1850 presentments many years ago as being of "no value".

Newspapers
Local newspapers contain recruiting advertisements and news about the local police. National newspapers have reports of legislation concerning the police and discussions about their place in society. There have been quite a number of such articles in recent years in newspapers like *The Times* or *The Guardian*. Back numbers can often be found in local reference libraries. There is a useful index to *The Times*.

Oral testimony
The record of what was actually said by people at the time, as recorded in newspapers, and evidence gathered by commissions like the Desborough Commission. Historians often interview people who lived through the time concerned and include their testimony in their books. The testimonies of Chief Inspector Bond and Glenys Campling used in this book are examples of this.

Parliamentary records
Records of parliamentary debates provide important information about the history of the police service and the social background. These can be found on the *Rolls of Parliament* (medieval), *Commons Journals* (sixteenth and seventeenth centuries), *Parliamentary Blue Books* (eighteenth and nineteenth centuries) and *Hansard* (since 1909). All these are stored in the Public Records Office in London, as are the records of the special commissions like the Desborough Commission. Acts of Parliament are published in volumes called *Statutes of the Realm*. Many reference libraries carry shortened versions, which are easier to use. Summaries of debates are often published in newspapers.

Pictorial evidence
Such as paintings and photographs. Cartoons show how people felt about the police.

Play and novels
Some works of fiction make references to the police of the time. The unwilling and incompetent constable is a stock comic figure in Shakespeare's plays.

Police records
Some police forces keep their own records, which may include policemen's notebooks, old correspondence and photographs, which give clues about the day-to-day work of that force. Some forces have produced their own histories, like that of East Sussex used in this book. The Metropolitan Police are opening a museum in South London in 1991-2.

Town and County Records
These are usually kept in the County Archive and include the records of the local watch or standing committees, including police finances. Portsmouth City Council have published a history of their police based on their records. There may be others.

Visual evidence
This is limited, but surviving police houses and older stations provide evidence about the organization of the police service after the 1840s and '50s.

Book List

a selection of interesting books on the history of the police

The Pioneer Policewoman   Mary Allen (Chatto and Windus, 1925)
The experiences of a suffragette and one of the first volunteer policewomen.

From Vine Street to Jerusalem   Joseph E. Broadbent (Stanley Paul, 1936)
A detective's story of his life in the Metropolitan (1899-1915) and Palestine police (1915-32).

A History of the Police in England and Wales   T.A. Critchley (Constable, 1975)
A detailed history of the police from Anglo-Saxon times. Deals mainly with the organization of the police but contains some information on their life and work.

A Day in the Life of a Victorian Policeman   John Garforth (Allen and Unwin, 1974) A reconstruction from the records of a typical day in the life of a London policeman of the 1840s.

The Story of Scotland Yard   Sir Ronald Hunter (Arthur Barker, 1965)
The story of the CID by a former head. Contains plenty of actual cases.

A Man Apart: The British Policeman and his Job   A. Judge (Arthur Barker, 1972)
A survey of the modern police force by an ex-policeman. Draws heavily on interviews.

The British policewoman: her story   Joan Locke (1979)
This book traces the struggles of the first policewomen 1914-45.

Spike Island   James McClure (Macmillan, 1980)
The author spent several weeks with A Division of the Merseyside Police, talking to them and watching them at work.

The Village Policeman   Ian Niall (Heinemann, 1971)
An intimate view of the life of a Welsh village policeman in the first half of this century, based on actual diaries.

Scotland Yard   John Deane Potter (Burke Publishing Company, 1972)
An account of the work of the CID, which includes much information on the history of forensic science and technology in solving crime.

Hue and Cry   P. Pringle (Museum Press, 1955)
The story of law and order in eighteenth-century London. Contains lots of material about the origins and early history of the Bow Street Runners.

Mr Punch and the Police   C. Pulling (Butterworth, 1964)
A collection of cartoons and skits from the popular satirical magazine, showing changing attitudes towards the police.

The British Police in a Changing Society   W. Purcell (Mowbray, 1974)
Interviews with policemen of all ranks and from different areas.

The Night the Police went on Strike   G.W. Reynolds and A. Judge (Weidenfeld, 1968) The story of the London police strike of 1918.

Coppers: An Inside View of the British Police   M. Seagrove (Harrap, 1967)
A personal account of three years in the Metropolitan Police in the early 1970s.

A Woman at Scotland Yard   Lilian Wyles (Faber and Faber, 1925)
One of the first regular Metropolitan Policewomen tells her story. She retired in 1949.

Timeline

PERIOD	DATES	SIGNIFICANT EVENTS IN BRITAIN
Prehistoric	**Until AD 43**	**c. 4500 BC** Britain becomes an island. **c. 1700 BC** Bronze Age; metal-working begins. **c. 700 BC** Iron Age.
Roman	**43 AD to 410**	**43 AD** Roman invasion of Britain. **50 AD** Foundation of London. **60 AD** Revolt of Boudicca. **410 AD** End of Roman rule.
Anglo-Saxon	**410 to 1066**	**c. 450** First settlers from Europe arrive in Britain. **597** St Augustine's mission to convert Britain to Christianity. **793 onwards** Viking invasions begin. **886** Alfred of Wessex becomes King of most of England.
Medieval or Middle Ages	**1066 to 1485**	**1066** Norman conquest. **1086** Domesday survey. **1215** Magna Carta. **1348** First outbreak of the Great Plague. **1455-71** Wars of the Roses.
Tudor Age (sixteenth century)	**1485 to 1603**	**1485** Defeat of Richard III at Battle of Bosworth Field; accession of Henry VII. **1509-47** Reign of Henry VIII. **1533** Final break with Rome and foundation of Church of England. **1536** Dissolution of the monasteries. Union of England and Wales. **1558** Accession of Queen Elizabeth I. **c. 1580** Shakespeare begins to write his plays. **1588** Defeat of Spanish Armada. **1594** Poor harvests begin.
Stuart Age (seventeenth century)	**1603 to 1714**	**1603** Death of Queen Elizabeth; James VI of Scotland ascends English throne as James I. **1642** Civil War begins. **1649** Execution of Charles I: England becomes a Republic. **1653** Oliver Cromwell becomes Lord Protector. Commonwealth period begins. **1660** Restoration of the monarchy; Charles II. **1666** Great Fire of London. **1688** Overthrow of King James II in the "Glorious Revolution". **1707** Union of England and Scotland. **1714** Death of Queen Anne, last of the Stuart monarchs.

AD: (Anno Domini) In the Year of Our Lord   Century: a hundred years

SOCIAL AND LEGAL DEVELOPMENTS IN BRITAIN	THE POLICE
Tribal farming society.	Family responsibility.
England an occupied country; Roman law imposed. Scotland and Wales unconquered	Family and community responsibility for minor crimes. Roman army for major crimes in England.
Ninth century onwards written codes of law; organized system of local courts; *wergild*; trial by ordeal.	System of community responsibility – tythings and hundreds. Hue and cry. Sheriffs.
Gradual emergence of English language and culture. **1116** Assize of Clarendon introduces Jury system. **1360** Justices of Peace replace sheriffs as main props of law and order in the countryside. **Thirteenth century onwards** growth of towns.	**1066 to twelfth century** Frankpledge system of mutual responsibility. **Twelfth century onwards** Unpaid village constable. **1285** Statute of Winchester orders citizens to act as watchmen in towns.
1550s onwards Increased volume of social legislation. **1590s onwards** Increased economic hardship and vagrancy.	Village constables. JPs. Watchmen.
1650s Period of experiments in government. **1688** Power of Parliament and the wealthy landowners is established.	Village constables. JPs. Watchmen in towns. **1663** Paid watchmen in London, the Charlies. **1655-7** Major-Generals.

Timeline

Notes: c: (circa) around about that time   BC: Before Christ

PERIOD	DATES	SIGNIFICANT EVENTS IN BRITAIN
Eighteenth century	**1714-1800**	**1715** Jacobite rising under the "Old Pretender". **1738** Foundation of the Methodist religion. **1745** Jacobite rising under Bonnie Prince Charlie, the "Young Pretender". **1769** James Watt patents the steam engine. **1780** Gordon riots in London. **1783** Loss of American colonies. **1793** Wars with France begin, that are to last over twenty years.
Nineteenth century	**1800-1900**	**1812** Luddite riots. **1815** Napoleonic Wars end. **1819** Peterloo massacre. **1822** Robert Peel becomes Home Secretary. **1825** First railway opens between Stockton and Darlington. **1832** First Reform Bill. **1837** Accession of Queen Victoria. **1867** Fenians explode bomb at Clerkenwell. **1884** Third Reform Act gives vote to all male householders over 21.
Twentieth century	**1900 onwards**	**1901** Death of Queen Victoria. **1903** Suffragette movement founded. **1914-18** First World War. **1918** All men over 21 given the vote. **1922** Republic of Ireland (Eire) created. **1926** General strike. **1928** All women over 21 given the vote. **1929** Wall Street Crash; Great Depression begins. **1939-45** Second World War. **1968** "Troubles" begin in Northern Ireland. **1979** Mrs Thatcher becomes Prime Minister. **1981** Riots in Toxteth and Brixton. **1984-5** Miners' strike.